SECRET BIRMINGHAM

A Guide to the Weird, Wonderful, and Obscure

Cherith Glover Fluker

Reedy Press
PO Box 5131
St. Louis, MO 63139
reedypress.com

Library of Congress Control Number: 2025936744
ISBN: 9781681066127

Design by Jill Halpin

Unless otherwise indicated, all photos are courtesy of the author or in the public domain.

Printed in the United States of America
25 26 27 28 29   5 4 3 2 1

To my mom and dad, who sparked my love for Birmingham, and to those who continue to believe in the magic of this incredible city.

Japanese Garden

CONTENTS

Photo courtesy of Wally Argus

ACKNOWLEDGMENTS

Writing a book has always been a dream of mine, but I never imagined my first book would be about Birmingham. This journey has deepened my love for the Magic City and transformed my life in ways I never expected. Though I've lived less than an hour away my entire life, the past year has uncovered layers of Birmingham I never knew existed. I've explored hidden corners of the city and met remarkable people I might never have encountered otherwise.

To everyone who shared secrets with me—or pointed me toward someone who could—I am deeply grateful. Special recognition goes to the Homewood Public Library for introducing me to its local history room, where countless hours of research unearthed many of the stories in this book. To everyone who agreed to be interviewed and generously shared their insights, thank you for trusting me with your time and knowledge.

I owe so much to Javacia Harris Bowser, one of the first to push me toward my writing dreams, and to the See Jane Write Collective for cheering me on every step of the way. My sisters—Marcia, Sabrina, and TaShawna—have been a constant source of support, patiently listening to updates and always making me feel like my stories were exciting.

I'm also grateful to my Reedy Press family for their encouragement and belief in this project.

To Birmingham itself: Thank you for being endlessly magical and for making the challenge of deciding what to include and what to leave out such a rewarding struggle.

To my biggest supporters—Cordell, Jordan, and Kaylen—your love and encouragement have meant everything to me. You listened to my endless stories and even joined me in wandering Birmingham's streets. I couldn't have done this without you. You are, without question, my MVPs.

Lastly, to my beautiful angels in Heaven—Mom and Dad. You always told me I could do anything I set my mind to, and time and again, your words have proven true. I love you, and I carry your guidance and love with me always.

Photo courtesy of Wally Argus

INTRODUCTION

The Magic City, that's Birmingham. This city, the heartbeat of Alabama, sparkles with a charm that is undeniable. From its rich history to its rapid growth, Birmingham is a place where the past and present collide to create a unique rhythm that continues to captivate locals and attract visitors. But sometimes, in the hustle and bustle of this thriving metropolis, it's easy to overlook the hidden gems that make Birmingham truly extraordinary.

Over the past year, I've taken the time to slow down and look more closely, exploring corners of the city that often go unnoticed. I've learned that the city's many popular destinations and attractions possess hidden qualities that could surprise even the most knowledgeable local. What I discovered is a collection of stories, places, and experiences that add layers of depth to Birmingham's already vibrant character. Even as a longtime friend of the city, I was amazed by the secrets it holds—secrets that reveal themselves only when you take the time to look beyond the surface.

Birmingham's history is as rich as the iron ore that built it, and its evolution tells a story of tenacity, creativity, and growth. What started out as an industrial powerhouse has transformed to its current status as an epicenter for innovation, culture, and community. Birmingham's spirit remains as dynamic as ever. And while its progress is exciting, it's the quiet, tucked-away wonders that remind us of the very soul of this city.

In *Secret Birmingham*, I give you the key to unlock the city's hidden magic. Whether you're a lifelong resident or a first-time visitor, there's something here for everyone. So let's take a closer look, explore the paths less traveled, and celebrate the sparkle that makes Birmingham shine in ways you may have never imagined.

WELCOME TO THE MAGIC CITY

What's the story behind Birmingham's iconic Magic City Rotary Trail sign?

For nearly a century, the Magic City sign has stood as an iconic symbol of Birmingham's history and resilience. The sign originally welcomed visitors to the city as they arrived at Birmingham's Terminal Station. It has undergone several transformations over the years. Each change marks a significant chapter in Birmingham's story.

The original sign was erected in 1926 at the west end of Fifth Avenue North. It read, "Welcome to Birmingham, the Magic City." As Birmingham evolved through decades of industrial growth and social change, the sign remained a constant, although it shifted in appearance and location.

By the 1950s, the sign had deteriorated and was eventually deemed a hazard and removed. Despite its physical absence, the sentiment and significance of the Magic City motto persisted in the hearts of Birmingham residents.

In recent years, the Magic City sign has been resurrected. It serves as a reminder of Birmingham's past while embracing its future. Now located along the Rotary Trail, the sign welcomes locals and visitors to walking paths, benches, and boardwalks. It is a testament to urban renewal and community spirit. The sign's relocation is an example of Birmingham's commitment to preserving its heritage.

MAGIC CITY ROTARY TRAIL SIGN

WHAT: Iconic sign at the entrance of the downtown Rotary Trail

WHERE: 2098 First Ave. S

COST: Free

PRO TIP: Visit during the evening hours when the sign is illuminated.

The original Magic City sign was removed in the 1950s due to deterioration. A restored version now proudly marks the entrance to the Rotary Trail in downtown Birmingham.

The Magic City sign, in all its iterations, symbolizes resilience, innovation, and the enduring spirit of a city that has weathered storms and emerged stronger. It represents the evolution from an industrial powerhouse to a cultural hub.

The modern version of the Magic City sign replicates the vintage style of the original sign, paying tribute to Birmingham's industrial boom and nickname as "The Magic City." The Magic City sign has evolved much like Birmingham—from a 1926 railway welcome to a symbol of urban renewal on the Rotary Trail.

WHERE VETERANS DAY WAS BORN

How did Veterans Day become a national holiday?

Veterans Day is a national holiday recognizing all who have served in the American armed forces. While this fact is widely known, many are unaware that Veterans Day originated right here in Birmingham.

World War I officially ended with the Treaty of Versailles, but the actual fighting had stopped seven months earlier, when a truce between the Allied nations and Germany began on the 11th hour of the 11th day of the 11th month.

In November 1919, President Woodrow Wilson proclaimed November 11 as the inaugural Armistice Day. As he addressed the nation, he praised the heroism of those who had perished in service and expressed gratitude for the victory that enabled America to advocate for peace and justice globally.

Initially, Armistice Day honored veterans of World War I. But after World War II, which saw the largest mobilization of soldiers, sailors, Marines, and airmen in US history, Raymond Weeks, a World War II veteran from Birmingham, suggested expanding Armistice Day to celebrate all veterans.

In 1947, Weeks went to Washington, DC, with a group to ask then-Army Chief of Staff General Dwight Eisenhower to create a national holiday for all veterans. In 1954, President Eisenhower signed a law making November 11 Veterans Day.

If you have time in your schedule, you might also want to take the 12-mile drive to the Alabama Veterans Memorial Park. It offers an inspiring tribute to the sacrifices of American veterans.

This monument in Linn Park pays tribute to the man whose dedication helped establish a national day to recognize and celebrate America's veterans. Courtesy of Mark Hilton (HMdb.org)

In 1982, President Ronald Reagan honored Weeks with the Presidential Citizens Medal, calling him the driving force behind Veterans Day. Weeks started the first National Veterans Day Parade in 1947 in Birmingham, and he kept organizing it until he passed away in 1985. Weeks is now honored by a memorial in Linn Park.

RAYMOND WEEKS MEMORIAL MONUMENT

WHAT: Monument honoring Raymond Weeks, the founder of Veterans Day

WHERE: Linn Park, 710 20th St. N

COST: Free

PRO TIP: Every Veterans Day, ceremonies are held at the Raymond Weeks Memorial Monument to remember his contributions.

WORLD'S LARGEST CAST IRON STATUE

Why is there an iron man overlooking Birmingham?

If you've ever visited Birmingham, you've likely seen the huge, cast iron, bare-bottomed man towering over the city. The Vulcan statue stands atop Red Mountain and is a striking symbol of the city's industrial heritage.

Standing at 56 feet tall, Vulcan is the largest cast iron statue in the world. The statue was designed by Italian sculptor Giuseppe Moretti and cast from local iron in 1904 to represent Birmingham at the St. Louis World's Fair, a significant event that showcased the cultural and industrial achievements of various cities. At the fair, Vulcan won the grand prize, bringing international recognition to Birmingham's booming iron and steel industry.

VULCAN PARK AND MUSEUM

WHAT: The world's largest cast iron statue

WHERE: 1701 Valley View Dr.

COST: Admission fee varies

PRO TIP: Visit the park in the late afternoon to enjoy stunning sunset views from the observation tower.

The Vulcan Center is a favorite destination for school field trips and a sought-after venue for hosting events. Courtesy of Vulcan Park and Museum

Standing tall over Birmingham, Vulcan symbolizes the city's industrial roots and enduring spirit. Courtesy of Vulcan Park and Museum

Vulcan, the Roman god of fire and forge, fittingly symbolizes the city's roots in iron and steel production. After the fair, the statue was relocated to Birmingham, a move that signified the city's growing prominence in the industrial sector. Initially set up at the Alabama State Fairgrounds, the statue was a testament to Birmingham's rapid industrial growth. In 1936, Vulcan found a permanent home atop Red Mountain.

Over the years, Vulcan has undergone several restorations, the most significant being completed in 2004, ensuring its status as a prominent landmark. Today, Vulcan is a major tourist attraction. From the statue's observation tower, visitors can enjoy panoramic views of the city. The Vulcan Park and Museum provides educational exhibits about the statue's history and Birmingham's industrial development. The park and statue are a centerpiece of local culture and history.

While you're at Vulcan Park, save some time to hike Vulcan Park's Mine Trail. It's a short but scenic hiking trail that takes visitors through a historic mining area near the statue.

LADY LIBERTY OVERLOOKING LIBERTY PARK

Why is there a Statue of Liberty replica in Birmingham?

As you drive along I-459 in Birmingham, you might spot an unexpected and intriguing landmark: a replica of the Statue of Liberty. This bronze statue, located in Liberty Park, tells a story that connects local business history with national symbolism. It is a unique and fascinating point of interest.

The story of Birmingham's Statue of Liberty replica begins in the 1950s when Frank Park Samford, founder of Liberty National Life Insurance Company, commissioned the statue. He wanted it to reflect the company's commitment to the ideals of freedom and liberty. Originally, the statue was placed atop the Liberty National Life Insurance building in downtown Birmingham.

On July 4, 1989, the statue was moved to Liberty Park as part of a development plan to make it more accessible to the public. Standing 36 feet tall on a 60-foot pedestal, this replica is about one-fifth the size of the original in New York Harbor. Its relocation to a serene park setting has only enhanced its appeal.

Birmingham's replica of the Statue of Liberty originally stood on the Liberty National Life Insurance building in downtown Birmingham. It was relocated to its current site on July 4, 1989.

The Statue of Liberty Replica has been a part of Birmingham's story since 1958. It was moved to its current location, right off Interstate 459, in 1989. Courtesy of Wally Argus

This replica is not just a quirky landmark; it's also a nod to the innovative spirit of Frank Park Samford. For residents and visitors alike, it serves as a reminder of the city's distinctive place in the American narrative.

THE STATUE OF LIBERTY REPLICA

WHAT: A replica of the Statue of Liberty

WHERE: Liberty Park, 516 Liberty Pkwy., Vestavia Hills

COST: Free

PRO TIP: Visit in the early morning or late afternoon for the best lighting for photos, and take a moment to read the plaque that details the statue's history and significance.

A SYMBOL OF INDUSTRIAL GROWTH

How can an old iron factory reveal the hidden essence of Birmingham?

"Sloss Furnaces is Birmingham's best-kept secret," says Tyler Malugani, education coordinator for Sloss. While many people have seen or heard of this landmark, few truly understand the rich history that lies within.

SLOSS FURNACES

WHAT: A historic industrial site transformed into an outdoor museum, event space, and arts facility

WHERE: Sloss Industrial District

COST: Free to tour museum; paid guided tours available. Special ticketed events throughout the year.

PRO TIP: Dress for the weather, wear comfortable shoes, and bring a water bottle. The site is expansive and requires a fair amount of walking.

Sloss Furnaces is one of the few remaining 20th-century blast furnaces preserved as a historic industrial site. Founded in 1881 by James Withers Sloss, the furnace played a pivotal role in the post–Civil War industrial boom of the Southern United States. It significantly contributed to Birmingham's emergence as an industrial powerhouse, earning the city the nickname "The Magic City."

Many Birmingham residents have a personal connection to Sloss Furnaces through family members who worked there, cementing its place in the local heritage. The site's history is a testament to the labor and lives of those who powered the iron industry. Many were black workers who faced harsh conditions and low wages yet were integral to the furnace's operations.

Today, Sloss Furnaces operates as a National Historic Landmark and museum. It offers a rare glimpse into the iron-

Sloss Furnaces was once a bustling hub of iron production. It is now a unique site for history, art, and events.

making industry and its profound impact on the region's economy and society. Sloss houses unique industrial equipment that can't be seen anywhere else in the country. In fact, it's one of only three museums of its kind in the world.

In addition to its historical and educational offerings, Sloss Furnaces hosts a variety of cultural events, art workshops, and even ghost tours. Throughout the year, it serves as a venue for weddings, music festivals, charity fundraisers, corporate events, and more. Sloss provides a unique and historically rich backdrop for a wide range of activities enjoyed by both residents and visitors alike.

Sloss Furnaces offers thrilling night tours that take visitors on a chilling journey through the site after dark.

WORLD'S LARGEST MOTORCYCLE MUSEUM

Where can you find the most extensive collection of motorcycles and racecars?

In 2014, Guinness World Records crowned Barber Vintage Motorsports Museum as the world's largest motorcycle museum. Located just 20 miles from downtown Birmingham, the museum is home to a collection of over 1,800 motorcycles and racing cars.

This museum captures the essence of motorsports history through its extraordinary collection and unique offerings. Barber's impressive collection includes pieces from 220 manufacturers across 22 countries, which makes it an international showcase of engineering and design excellence.

George W. Barber, a former racecar driver with a passion for both cars and motorcycles, founded the museum in 1995. And this museum is not just a static display; nearly all the motorcycles can be run within an hour. The museum is dedicated to maintaining these machines in top condition.

One of the most unique aspects of the Barber Vintage Motorsports Museum is its integration with the Barber Motorsports Park. This 880-acre facility includes a world-

Barber Vintage Motorsports Museum is listed in the Guinness Book of World Records as being the world's largest motorcycle museum. Courtesy of Chuck Schulze

Courtesy of Jamie Martin

class 2.38-mile racetrack that hosts numerous automotive events, such as the Porsche Track Experience and the Indy Grand Prix of Alabama. The park was designed with input from renowned racers and is considered one of the most beautiful racetracks globally, combining the thrill of racing with stunning natural scenery.

While the museum is widely known for its motorcycle collection, it also boasts the world's most extensive collection of Lotus racecars. Additionally, it features a research library and an advanced design center. It is truly a center for motorsports innovation and education.

Visitors to the museum can expect to see an exceptional collection of motorcycles and cars and experience the living history of motorsports in a setting that beautifully merges the past and present.

BARBER VINTAGE MOTORSPORTS MUSEUM

WHAT: The world's largest motorcycle museum

WHERE: 6030 Barber Motorsports Pkwy.

COST: Fee for admission

PRO TIP: Consider a Premium Museum Tour for exclusive access.

The museum showcases legendary race cars like the 1964 Ferrari F-158, driven by John Surtees to win the 1964 Formula 1 World Championship.

THE HEAVIEST CORNER ON EARTH

What makes a city corner the "Heaviest Corner on Earth"?

At the intersection of 20th Street North and First Avenue North stand four buildings: the Woodward Building, the Brown Marx Building, the John A. Hand Building, and the Empire Building (now the Elyton Hotel). This corner earned the nickname "Heaviest Corner on Earth" due to the significant heights and masses of these structures, each a landmark in Birmingham's early 20th-century skyline.

In 1911, *Jemison* magazine proclaimed Birmingham to have the heaviest corner in the South, highlighting the completion of these four monumental buildings. At the time, these skyscrapers were among the tallest structures in the American South, solidifying Birmingham's flourishing skyline.

The story begins with the 10-story Woodward Building. It was completed in 1902. This Chicago-style structure, with its steel-frame construction, was Birmingham's first of its kind. William Woodward invested in creating this 132-foot architectural marvel designed by William Weston.

HEAVIEST CORNER ON EARTH

WHAT: A collection of towering historic skyscrapers

WHERE: Intersection of 20th St. N and First Ave. N

COST: Free

PRO TIP: Capture a lasting memory by snapping photos of the sidewalk plaques and the National Historical Marker that commemorate the significance and architectural grandeur of this iconic Birmingham landmark.

This corner in Birmingham got its name in the early 20th century due to the concentration of tall, weighty skyscrapers built there within a short period of time.

Next came the Brown Marx Building in 1906. It is known for its arched windows and significant stature. This building once housed the United States Steel Corporation.

In 1909, the 247-foot Empire Building was completed. Its neoclassical design and multi-use purpose made it a cornerstone of the city's business district. Over the years, the Empire Building has undergone several transformations, becoming the Elyton Hotel in 2017.

The final piece of the puzzle was the John Hand Building. It was completed in 1912 and originally named the American Trust and Savings Bank Building. This 21-story structure claimed the title of the tallest building in Alabama, cementing the corner's nickname.

In 1985, the corner's nickname was made official, complete with a plaque installed by the Birmingham Historical Society. The quartet of buildings was also included on the National Register of Historic Places.

Today, the Heaviest Corner on Earth remains a testament to Birmingham's architectural and economic ambitions, inviting visitors to marvel at its storied past and towering presence.

The Elyton Hotel retains many of the Empire Building's original architectural elements. The vintage bank vaults are still in place, paying homage to its rich history in the financial industry.

URBAN NATURE PRESERVE

Where in Birmingham can you take a hike, enjoy scenic views, and explore historic mining sites?

Birmingham is home to one of the largest urban nature preserves in the United States. Ruffner Mountain, located between Birmingham and Irondale, encompasses over 1,000 acres of urban forest and natural landscape.

Visitors can explore more than 12 miles of trails, which offer a variety of experiences from rocky overlooks to wetland boardwalks and remnants of Birmingham's mining past. The Tree House, the name for the preserve's visitor center, opened in 2010 and features a unique living plant roof. It serves as an informational and educational space that hosts exhibits on native wildlife. Meeting spaces are also available in the center.

Ruffner Mountain Nature Preserve was named after William Henry Ruffner, a geologist who mapped the region's iron ore deposits. Remains of Birmingham's mining history can be found throughout the preserve. Sloss Iron and Steel Company operated mines on the mountain from the late 1880s until 1953. After the mines closed, the area began to recover naturally. In the 1970s, local groups saved 28 acres from development, forming the nonprofit Ruffner Mountain Nature Coalition to manage the preserve. This effort was supported

---

The Quarry Trail is the most popular trail at Ruffner Mountain for seeing ruins. Along this moderate, 3-mile trail, you'll see an abandoned limestone quarry, old mining equipment, and the Ruffner No. 2 mine entrance.

The Nature Center at Ruffner Mountain Nature Preserve features exhibits on local flora, fauna, and geology. Courtesy of Wally Argus

by donations and partnerships, and eventually the preserve was expanded to its present size.

In addition to scenic trails and breathtaking overlooks, the preserve also offers a range of educational programs aligned with state curriculum standards for K-12 students and serves as an outdoor classroom for higher education. It also focuses on conservation efforts, including invasive plant removal and wildlife habitat enhancement.

RUFFNER MOUNTAIN NATURE PRESERVE

WHAT: The nation's second-largest urban nature preserve

WHERE: 1214 81st St. S

COST: Fee for a parking permit

PRO TIP: Make sure to check out the trail map and choose a trail that matches your interests and fitness level.

SYMBOL OF THE CIVIL RIGHTS MOVEMENT

How did a single act of violence at a historic church in Birmingham become a defining moment in the fight for civil rights?

On Sunday morning, September 15, 1963, dozens of unsuspecting churchgoers filed into the 16th Street Baptist Church in Birmingham, ready for a regular worship service. The church, a prominent beacon of unity in the black community, had long been a gathering place for those seeking solace and strength amidst the tumultuous Civil Rights Movement. However, on this particular day, the church would become the site of one of the most horrific and historic attacks of the era.

As the congregation settled into their pews, the sound of hymns and prayers filled the air. Little did they know that the tranquility of their worship was about to be shattered by an act of unthinkable violence. At 10:22 a.m., a bomb planted by members of the Ku Klux Klan detonated, ripping through the church's basement. The blast sent shock waves through the building, and news of it quickly spread throughout the nation.

16TH STREET BAPTIST CHURCH

WHAT: First black church in Birmingham and symbol of the civil rights movement

WHERE: 1530 Sixth Ave. N

COST: Fee for tours

PRO TIP: Check the church's schedule for guided tours and special events.

The 16th Street Baptist Church is one of seven sites that are part of the Birmingham Civil Rights National Monument.

Left: *16th Street Baptist Church is credited with being the first black church in the city. Courtesy of Carol Highsmith*

Below: *Inside the historic 16th Street Baptist Church. Courtesy of Art Meripol*

The bombing claimed the lives of four young girls: Addie Mae Collins, Denise McNair, Carole Robertson, and Cynthia Wesley. These girls, dressed in their Sunday best, had been preparing for the church's annual Youth Day service, completely unaware of the hatred that had targeted them. The explosion reduced the church's interior to rubble, but the community's spirit remained unbroken.

The tragedy of the 16th Street Baptist Church bombing became a pivotal moment in the Civil Rights Movement, drawing national and international attention to the brutal realities of racial segregation and violence in America. The loss of these four little girls galvanized activists and spurred legislative changes. Shortly after this incident, the Civil Rights Act of 1964 was passed.

Today, the 16th Street Baptist Church stands as a place of worship and a symbol of resilience. For many, it is a reminder of the sacrifices made in the pursuit of justice and equality. Visitors can walk through its halls and reflect on the legacy of those who perished and the enduring fight for civil rights that continues to shape the nation.

OLDEST BASEBALL PARK IN AMERICA

Where can you walk the same grounds as baseball legends like Babe Ruth and Willie Mays?

In the West End of Birmingham, you'll find a living relic of America's pastime: Rickwood Field. This historic baseball field proudly holds the title of the oldest baseball park in America. Named after its founder, Rick Woodward, Rickwood Field welcomed 10,000 fans for its inaugural game on August 18, 1910, featuring the Birmingham Barons, a team that still thrives today.

Many notable baseball greats have played on Rickwood's hallowed grounds, including Babe Ruth, Ty Cobb, Dizzy Dean, and Willie Mays. You might also have caught a glimpse of Rickwood Field in movies like *Cobb*, *Soul of the Game*, and *42*.

Rickwood Field's significance runs deep into African American history. During the segregation era, it was the home of the Birmingham Black Barons, a Negro League team that showcased extraordinary talent. This rich heritage is honored annually during the Rickwood Classic, where the Barons don vintage uniforms and the ballpark comes alive with the spirit of a bygone era.

RICKWOOD FIELD

WHAT: America's first baseball field

WHERE: 1137 Second Ave. W

COST: Free self-guided tours. Guided tours are available.

PRO TIP: Take a guided tour to fully appreciate the rich history of the stadium.

Rickwood Field has been on the National Register of Historic Places since 1993.

Rickwood Field is the oldest baseball park in America. It is the former home of the Birmingham Barons and the Black Barons. Photos courtesy of Rickwood Field

In 2024, Rickwood Field celebrated its rich history by hosting a grand event marking the 100th anniversary of the Negro Leagues, drawing visitors and players from across the country to honor the legacy of these groundbreaking athletes.

Today, Rickwood Field continues to be a cultural hub, hosting various community gatherings. Its timeless charm attracts baseball enthusiasts and history buffs alike to enjoy a nostalgic journey through the golden age of baseball.

Guided tours of Rickwood Field are available, giving visitors a deeper dive into its past and enabling them to walk the same grounds as the legends. Visiting Rickwood is like stepping into a living museum. Whether you're a local or a visitor, Rickwood Field is a must-see, a place where history and sport intertwine.

BIRMINGHAM'S OLDEST HOTEL

Did you know that Birmingham has a 100-year-old hotel?

Standing proudly since 1925, the Redmont Hotel is Birmingham's oldest and longest-running hotel. Designed by renowned architect G. Lloyd Preacher, the hotel has seen a century of history unfold around it.

While the Redmont has been restored and modernized, its exterior remains virtually unchanged. Every effort was made to preserve its vintage charm. The commitment to its historic character has earned the hotel a place on the National Register of Historic Places.

Inside, the hotel blends historic elegance with contemporary comfort. Upon entering, guests are welcomed by a massive

The Redmont Hotel was once a favorite hangout for celebrities and dignitaries passing through Birmingham. It has hosted a variety of notable guests, like Hank Williams and Kareem Abdul-Jabbar.

chandelier. Between the elevator doors, the original mail chute still stands. It serves as a subtle reminder of a time when letters and telegrams were the height of communication. On the rooftop, a large neon sign stands as an iconic part of Birmingham's skyline.

Named after Birmingham's Red Mountain, this luxurious hotel was the first in the city to offer private bathrooms. Its halls, many of which are rumored to be haunted, have whispered countless stories. Numerous sources claim that Hank Williams Sr. spent his last night alive here. The "Lucky Governors Suite" got its name from two Alabama governors who launched their successful campaigns from within the hotel walls: George Wallace and Jim Folsom.

Unlike many hotels that skip the 13th floor due to superstitions, the Redmont Hotel includes it. This decision adds to the hotel's unique character and has become a point of intrigue for guests.

With its classic charm and rich history, the Redmont Hotel is more than a place to stay—it's a vibrant part of Birmingham's legacy that keeps adding to the city's story.

REDMONT HOTEL

WHAT: Birmingham's oldest and longest-running hotel

WHERE: 2101 Fifth Ave. N

COST: Check website for current rates.

PRO TIP: The hotel's central location puts you within easy reach of Birmingham's top attractions, dining, and entertainment.

This historic hotel is the oldest hotel in Birmingham still in use. Courtesy of Wally Argus

FROM RAILROAD DEPOT TO HISTORICAL HUB

How can you learn about Bessemer's industrial past?

The Bessemer Hall of History, located less than 20 miles from the heart of Birmingham, is a hidden gem that encapsulates the often overlooked history of the "Marvel City." Housed in a former railroad depot built in 1916, the museum is more than just a collection of artifacts—it's a living testament to Bessemer's past.

BESSEMER HALL OF HISTORY MUSEUM

WHAT: A museum dedicated to the history of Bessemer, Alabama

WHERE: 1905 Alabama Ave., Bessemer

COST: Free

PRO TIP: Set aside time to chat with the staff or volunteers—they often share fascinating local stories and insights that aren't in the exhibits.

The building is a relic from a time when Bessemer, like Birmingham, was a thriving industrial center. The railroad depot once served as a vital connection point that fueled the city's rapid growth. Today, it stands as a gateway to a treasure trove of local history. Visitors can step back in time and explore the origins of this resilient community.

Inside, the museum showcases an array of exhibits that tell the story of Bessemer's development, from its founding by industrialist Henry Fairchild DeBardeleben in the late 19th century to its role in the steel industry and beyond. One of the standout displays is dedicated to the city's railway history. It features authentic telegraph equipment, conductor uniforms, and even a restored railway car. These exhibits paint a picture of an era when the railroad was the heartbeat of Bessemer's economy.

Learn all about Bessemer's industrial past in this railroad depot turned history museum. Courtesy of Wally Argus

The Bessemer Hall of History isn't just a repository of the past; it's also said to be a hotspot for paranormal activity. According to local lore, the museum is haunted by the spirits of those who once passed through its doors during its days as a bustling railway depot. Visitors and staff alike have reported eerie occurrences, including the sound of footsteps echoing through empty halls and doors that inexplicably open and close on their own. Some have even claimed to see shadowy figures near the old ticket counter, thought to be the lingering presence of passengers who never left. These tales add a chilling and fascinating layer to the museum's already rich historical tapestry.

For anyone interested in uncovering the lesser-known stories of Birmingham's surrounding areas, the Bessemer Hall of History is a must-visit destination. It's a place where the echoes of the past are preserved, waiting to be discovered by those curious enough to look.

Visitors to the Bessemer Hall of History can walk next door and step aboard the one-millionth Pullman rail car ever built. It is a fascinating piece of history that symbolizes the city's ties to the railroad industry.

ITALIAN TEMPLE IN BIRMINGHAM

Where can you find a Roman architectural icon near Birmingham?

Sibyl Temple sits at the summit of Shades Crest Road in Vestavia Hills. It is a shining piece of classical architecture that has a lot of history. This elegant structure, inspired by the ancient Temple of Sibyl in Tivoli, Italy, was commissioned by former Birmingham mayor George B. Ward in 1929. Ward, known for his eccentric fascination with classical antiquity, wanted to re-create the grandeur of Roman architecture on his estate, Vestavia, which already featured a grand villa designed in the style of a Roman temple.

The temple initially served as a gazebo where guests could admire the rolling landscapes of the Birmingham area. Built with pristine white marble and supported by Corinthian columns, Sibyl Temple quickly became an icon of Southern sophistication and romanticism. Its location provided a view that enhanced its ethereal presence.

SIBYL TEMPLE

WHAT: A classical marble structure inspired by the ancient Temple of Sibyl in Italy

WHERE: 154 Montgomery Hwy., Vestavia Hills

COST: Free

PRO TIP: Visit Sibyl Temple at sunset for stunning panoramic views of the Birmingham area.

Sibyl Temple is one of many landmarks in the area that offer historical significance and scenic beauty.

After Ward's death and the subsequent sale of his estate, the temple was relocated in 1976 to its current site, where it was opened to the public as part of a city park. Today, it serves not only as a popular spot for weddings and events but also as a serene overlook where visitors can experience a piece of Birmingham's cultural and architectural history.

Sibyl Temple, one of Vestavia Hills' top tourist attractions, is a popular location for weddings, photography, and small gatherings. Courtesy of Curtis Palmer

BIRMINGHAM'S OLDEST RESCUE MISSION

Which prominent figure is memorialized with a statue in Five Points South?

Reverend James Alexander "Brother" Bryan was a beloved community leader in the city. He was known for his lifelong dedication to helping the city's homeless population. As the founder of the Brother Bryan Mission, he provided food, shelter, and compassion to those in need. He always referred to everyone he met as "brother" or "sister" to emphasize his belief in equality and kindness. His work had a profound impact on the city, and he is remembered for his selflessness and devotion to the less fortunate.

In 1934, a statue was built to honor him. It was originally located at the Brother Bryan Prayer Point on Red Mountain but was later moved to its current location in Five Points South, a lively district known for its dining, shopping, and cultural significance. The statue was funded by public donations from Birmingham residents who wanted to honor Brother Bryan's contributions to the community. This act of generosity reflects the deep admiration the people of Birmingham had for Bryan and his mission.

The Mission continues to serve the homeless community today. It offers emergency shelter, food, and resources to those in need. Its impact is still felt throughout the city as it provides a vital lifeline for those experiencing hardship.

The Brother Bryan statue is notable because it depicts the pastor kneeling in prayer, symbolizing his dedication to faith and service.

BROTHER BRYAN STATUE

WHAT: A white marble sculpture of the Reverend James Alexander Bryan, also known as Brother Bryan, a well-known pastor in Birmingham

WHERE: 20th St. S and Magnolia Ave.

COST: Free

PRO TIP: While you're there, explore the surrounding area in Five Points South. This historic neighborhood is filled with local restaurants, cafés, and unique shops.

This marble statue of Brother Bryan was moved twice before returning to Five Points South, where it remains today.

The statue not only honors Brother Bryan's vision but also serves as a reminder of the importance of compassion and community service in shaping the city's identity. It is a powerful symbol of how one person's dedication can continue to inspire and uplift a community long after they're gone.

JAPANESE GARDEN IN BIRMINGHAM

JAPANESE GARDEN

WHAT: Part of the Birmingham Botanical Gardens, designed using traditional Japanese elements and architecture

WHERE: 2612 Lane Park Rd.

COST: Free

PRO TIP: Don't forget to walk through the moon bridge for a perfect photo spot!

Where can you find a Japanese-inspired garden in the heart of the city?

Inside Birmingham's botanical landscape is a serene escape: the Birmingham Botanical Gardens' Japanese Garden. The garden offers a peek into the art and aesthetics of Japanese horticulture. In fact, it is the only Japanese garden in Birmingham.

The garden was designed to emulate traditional Japanese landscapes and invites visitors to experience a slice of the East amid the Southern charm. In fact, once you cross the threshold, you might think you've stepped into another country.

Hitachi, Japan, one of Birmingham's sister cities, shares a long-standing bond with the city. The Japanese Garden is a symbol of that bond. The garden showcases elegant stone lanterns gifted by Hitachi. In return, Birmingham gifted Hitachi with a 10-foot replica of Birmingham's iconic Vulcan statue.

The garden is a beautiful combination of manicured

Once you step through the red torii at the Japanese Garden, you're instantly transported to a serene corner of Japan.

landscapes, koi-filled ponds, and arched bridges. Visitors can also engage with Japanese culture through a traditional tea ceremony at the garden's teahouse or by reflecting on the thoughtful Zen Buddhist principles incorporated into the design.

The garden offers a touch of Japan's culture, history, and aesthetics. It is a reminder of the cultural exchange that has long connected Birmingham and Hitachi.

The conservatory is another fascinating feature at Birmingham Botanical Gardens. This glass-enclosed structure houses a collection of tropical and desert plants, including exotic orchids, towering palms, and rare cacti.

HISTORIC MASONIC TEMPLE BUILDING

What building was the only place black people could do business in Birmingham during the Civil Rights Movement?

In the heart of Birmingham's historic 4th Avenue District stands a towering symbol of resilience and enterprise: the Colored Masonic Temple. Known as the "Black Skyscraper," this eight-story building, built in 1922, was the vision of African American architect Robert Robinson Taylor. The Colored Masonic Temple served as a beacon of hope and opportunity for Birmingham's black community during segregation.

The building was one of the most advanced black-owned buildings of its time. It housed an electric elevator, modern offices, a ballroom, a bank, retail shops, and a theater. As a key meeting place during the Civil Rights Movement, it played a crucial role in organizing efforts. Its blend of architectural innovation, economic empowerment, and historical significance made it a groundbreaking landmark in Birmingham.

It is said that the Colored Masonic Temple contained hidden passageways and back entrances which were used for discreet meetings during the Civil Rights Movement. Civil rights leaders, including Dr. Martin Luther King Jr. and other key figures, are believed to have gathered in the building to organize protests and strategy sessions. The Colored Masonic Temple was once the largest and most advanced facility ever built by African Americans.

This historic temple once served as the heart of black culture in segregated Birmingham.

COLORED MASONIC TEMPLE

WHAT: A historic building in Birmingham's 4th Avenue District that served as a business, social, and cultural hub for the black community during segregation

WHERE: 1630 Fourth Ave. N

COST: Free to visit but currently closed for inside tours.

PRO TIP: Plan time to explore the surrounding 4th Avenue Historic District, where you'll find markers and other historical landmarks that give context to Birmingham's rich civil rights history.

At a time when access to white-owned facilities was restricted, the building buzzed with entrepreneurial spirit. Its walls echoed with the aspirations of a community that was determined to succeed despite the barriers it faced. Not only was the Colored Masonic Temple significant in commerce—it was also a social and cultural hub where fraternal organizations met and where important community meetings and events were held.

One of the building's most notable features was the Booker T. Washington Library, the first library in Birmingham to lend books to black citizens.

Though the Colored Masonic Temple is currently unoccupied, it remains a cherished landmark in Birmingham's civil rights history. Tourists from near and far visit to reflect on the stories etched into its walls. It stands not only as a relic of segregation but also as a testament to the strength and perseverance of Birmingham's black community. The temple is a quiet yet powerful reminder that Birmingham's story is one of overcoming.

ROMANESQUE PLAYHOUSE AT CALDWELL PARK

What is Birmingham's oldest performing arts venue?

Tucked away in Caldwell Park, the Virginia Samford Theatre is a timeless piece of Birmingham's landscape. A Romanesque-style playhouse built in 1927, the theater originally opened its doors as the Little Theatre and was a community haven for live performances. Over the years, it evolved into the Clark Memorial Theatre and later the Town and Gown Theatre, all the while gaining a reputation for staging hundreds of first-rate productions.

The theater's history aligns with the resilience of Birmingham. During World War II, it was forced to close due to financial cutbacks and remained closed for nearly a decade. In 1950, the theater triumphantly reopened, and for the next 40 years, it became a popular venue for artistic expression, hosting plays, musicals, and cultural events that attracted audiences from all walks of life.

In the early 1960s, the lobby of the Virginia Samford Theatre became a piece of Hollywood movie history. It's where local kids Mary Badham and Philip Alford auditioned and landed the

VIRGINIA SAMFORD THEATRE

WHAT: A beautifully restored 1927 Romanesque-style theater

WHERE: 26th St. S

COST: Ticket prices vary depending on the performance. Discounts are often available for students, seniors, and groups.

PRO TIP: Arrive early and explore the scenic Caldwell Park right next to the theater. It's a great spot for a pre-show picnic or a relaxing walk. Also, the theater has limited parking, so arriving early will give you the best chance of finding a spot close to the entrance.

Courtesy of Tim Carr

roles of Scout and Jem in To Kill a Mockingbird. Their big break added a fun and unexpected twist to the theater's story. What started as just another community casting call turned into a major Hollywood moment for the theatre.

By 1999, the future of the historic building was once again in jeopardy. The University of Alabama at Birmingham announced plans to close the theater, leaving its fate uncertain. That's when the Metropolitan Arts Council stepped in, determined to restore the landmark to its former glory. Thanks to their efforts, the building underwent a major renovation. In 2002, it reopened with a new name—the Virginia Samford Theatre, honoring philanthropist Virginia Samford Donovan, whose generous donation helped make the restoration possible.

Today, the Virginia Samford Theatre continues to captivate audiences with its mix of contemporary and classic performances. Its rich history, paired with its beautifully restored Romanesque architecture, makes it a must-visit for both locals and history buffs. Each year, the theater attracts those seeking to enjoy a Broadway show, see a local production, or simply admire the theater's architectural charm.

The Virginia Samford Theatre has hosted a variety of popular productions, from *Les Misérables* to *The Sound of Music*. It's a great place to catch an amazing performance while sitting in a space full of history.

CENTURY-OLD LEGACY CAR DEALERSHIP

How has Edwards Chevrolet Company become part of Birmingham's history for over a century?

Edwards Chevrolet Company is a testament to resilience and tradition. This family legacy car dealership opened its doors on August 5, 1916. Founded by William Sterling Edwards Jr., the dealership has flourished for over a century and is one of the oldest Chevrolet dealerships in the Southeast.

William Edwards Jr. was not just an entrepreneur; he was a visionary who understood the needs of his community. Born and raised in Birmingham, he recognized the potential of the automobile industry. He established Edwards Chevrolet as a dealership where residents could find quality vehicles and reliable service. Over the years, the dealership has evolved with the changing times while maintaining its commitment to customer satisfaction and community service.

EDWARDS CHEVROLET COMPANY

WHAT: One of the oldest car dealerships in Alabama

WHERE: 1400 Third Ave. N

COST: Varies depending on selection

PRO TIP: Edwards Chevrolet opened its second location on Highway 280 in 2007.

What sets Edwards Chevrolet apart is its dedication to family values. Now in its third generation of family ownership, the dealership continues to embody the principles established by William Edwards Jr. His legacy lives on in the hands of his descendants, who share his passion for automobiles and commitment to their customers.

For many Birmingham residents, Edwards Chevrolet represents more than just a place to buy a car; it's a cherished part of their community's history. My own father sold cars there for over two decades, building lasting relationships with customers and friends alike. The familiar faces of loyal patrons speak to the dealership's enduring reputation for honesty and integrity.

As you step into Edwards Chevrolet, you're not just entering a car dealership; you're walking into a living history of Birmingham—a place where generations have come together to celebrate the joy of driving and the spirit of family.

Sterling Edwards used his entire savings, $6,000 to open Edwards Motor Company in 1916.

Edwards Chevrolet has been serving customers in the Birmingham area for over a century. Courtesy of Wally Argus

HISTORY ON A COBBLESTONE ROAD

Where can you walk along a cobblestone road in the heart of downtown Birmingham?

Time seems to stand still in the Morris Avenue Historic District. You can almost feel the pulse of history beneath your feet as you walk down its cobblestone street. Morris Avenue, named after one of the city's founders, Josiah Morris, offers a glimpse into Birmingham's past as it remains a bustling part of the city.

Morris played a pivotal role in shaping Birmingham. He secured the funds that established the city in 1871. The street that bears his name reflects the spirit of Birmingham's early industry. Morris Avenue was once lined with warehouses, cotton brokers, and wholesale grocers. Many of these 19th-century buildings still stand today and serve as a testament to the city's preservation efforts. These brick facades and iron shutters tell stories of Birmingham as a rapidly growing hub for industry and trade.

MORRIS AVENUE HISTORIC DISTRICT

WHAT: A preserved area featuring cobblestone streets and historic buildings from the late 19th century, reflecting the city's industrial heritage

WHERE: Between 18th St. S and 22nd St. N

COST: Free

PRO TIP: Be sure to carve out some time to stop by Mercantile on Morris, a charming collection of locally owned shops.

As you stroll along Morris Avenue, you can spot some of the city's oldest and most well-preserved structures. The Ideal Building, for example, stands out as one of the architectural gems from the early 1900s, showcasing Birmingham's growth during that era. In the 1970s, the district experienced a revitalization, with the old warehouses converted into offices,

Morris Avenue, one of Birmingham's oldest streets, was originally paved with Belgian blocks in the 1880s, many of which still remain today. Courtesy of Tim Carr

restaurants, and lofts, blending modern touches with the street's historic charm.

Today, Morris Avenue offers a mix of modern urban life and vintage appeal. It's a popular spot for locals and tourists alike. The street is known for its quirky shops, cozy cafés, and vibrant atmosphere. You will often see individuals, couples, and groups posing for photos along the cobblestone paths and picturesque alleys.

Both history buffs and passersby enjoy taking in the scenery on Morris Avenue. Here, you can step back in time and experience a side of Birmingham that continues to enchant visitors year after year.

A standout feature on Morris Avenue is the red caboose that appears to emerge from a building, enhancing the unique character of this historic block.

FIRST PUBLIC LIBRARY IN THE CITY

Where can you find your ancestors and study your family roots?

There are approximately 41 public libraries in and around Birmingham, but only one can wear the title of the first public library in the city: the Linn-Henley Research Library. The library is a quiet treasure that reveals Birmingham's rich history to those who seek it. This grand library has evolved into a center for knowledge and heritage. It offers a glimpse into the lives of Birmingham's founders and the people who built the city.

Originally named the Birmingham Public Library, it was later renamed to honor the Linn and Henley families, two of the city's most influential early families. When you step inside, you are welcomed by the library's stunning architecture. The building houses government publications, special collections, and an array of historical documents. One of the most captivating features is the series of beautiful murals that adorn its walls. Each mural is a visual narrative that celebrates the history of knowledge and the pursuit of learning. These vibrant works of art create an atmosphere of reflection and discovery. Seeing it in person surpasses any photos I've ever seen.

For those interested in genealogy, the Linn-Henley Research Library is a haven. Here, you can sift through records and resources to trace your ancestors and uncover the stories of your family roots. The library offers a reading room where

---

On your first visit, finding the entrance to the Linn-Henley Research Library might feel like uncovering a secret. Be sure to stop by the front desk for directions.

LINN-HENLEY RESEARCH LIBRARY

WHAT: Birmingham's first public library, renowned for its beautiful murals and quiet reading rooms

WHERE: 2100 Park Pl.

COST: Free

PRO TIP: Give yourself extra time to walk around and see the beautiful works of art inside the building.

The Linn-Henley Research Library stands as a beacon of learning and discovery in the heart of Birmingham.

you can immerse yourself in quiet study or personal exploration as you connect with Birmingham's past or research your own lineage.

The Linn-Henley Research Library is more than just a repository of books—it's a doorway to understanding the city's history, a peaceful retreat for research, and a celebration of Birmingham's cultural heritage.

JAZZ IN THE MAGIC CITY

How did Birmingham contribute to the development of jazz music?

Birmingham is often overlooked when it comes to jazz music, but it has contributed in many ways. A visit to the Alabama Jazz Hall of Fame located in the historic 4th Avenue District will give you a closer look at the depth of Alabama's jazz roots.

The Alabama Jazz Hall of Fame is often called a hidden jewel—a tribute to the rich legacy of jazz in the state. Those who step into the hall are treated to a celebration of the incredible contributions that Alabamians have made to the world of jazz music. As you explore the halls of the museum, you'll hear the sounds of jazz filling the space, an experience that's sure to transport you to another time.

With a purpose to preserve and honor the accomplishments of Alabama's jazz legends, the Hall of Fame showcases the stories and achievements of iconic musicians like Nat King Cole, Erskine Hawkins, and Sun Ra. It's not just a museum—it's a vibrant reminder of the cultural heritage that has shaped both Birmingham and jazz history.

ALABAMA JAZZ HALL OF FAME

WHAT: Museum recognizing Birmingham's contributions to jazz

WHERE: 1631 Fourth Ave. N

COST: Fee for admission

PRO TIP: Check the schedule for live performances and special events before your visit.

The Alabama Jazz Hall of Fame is small, but it is packed with information about Birmingham's contributions to jazz music.

The Alabama Jazz Hall of Fame is located inside the historic Carver Theatre in the 4th Avenue business district. Courtesy of Carol Highsmith

Located inside the Carver Theatre, the museum enables visitors to explore exhibits filled with instruments, memorabilia, and photos that paint a picture of the state's unique influence on jazz.

For Birmingham locals, the Alabama Jazz Hall of Fame offers a sense of pride and connection to the city's past, while out-of-town guests will find it a fascinating stop on their journey through the Magic City. Jazz enthusiasts and those looking to learn more about the genre will uncover cultural gems in this intimate must-visit site.

ALABAMA'S OLDEST RESTAURANT

Where can you enjoy a delicious meal while soaking in a historic venue?

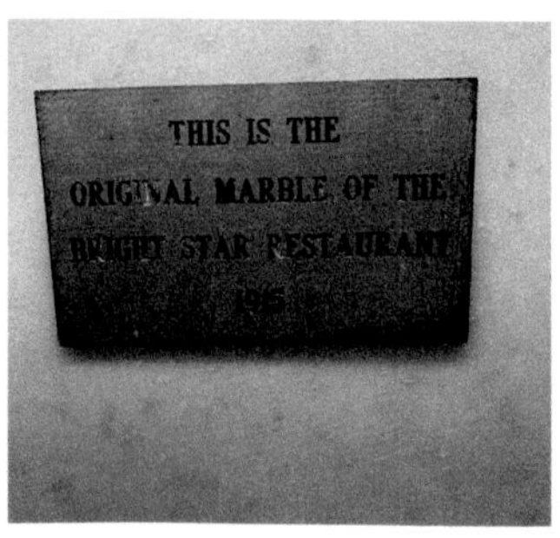

The Bright Star is one of Alabama's oldest restaurants.

A short southwest drive from downtown Birmingham will land you at the Bright Star Restaurant—Alabama's oldest restaurant. It stands as a culinary gem, cherished by locals and visitors for its rich history and delectable offerings. The Bright Star was established in 1907, and it won't take you long to see why this establishment has captured the hearts of so many people. As you approach, the iconic sign grabs your attention with a warm glow, promising a welcoming atmosphere and an unforgettable dining experience.

The original owner of the restaurant was Tom Bonduris. His cousins, Peter and Bill Koikos, who immigrated from the same small village in Greece, later became co-owners. Today, the restaurant is owned by Nicky Koikos, Andreas Annastassakis, and Stacey Craig.

The Bright Star is renowned for its seafood, particularly the Greek-style snapper and shrimp, which have become staples for both long-time patrons and newcomers. Other popular dishes include the deliciously tender prime rib and the house salad with a tangy homemade dressing, all of which reflect the restaurant's commitment to quality and tradition.

The Bright Star has been serving customers since 1907.

THE BRIGHT STAR

WHAT: Alabama's oldest restaurant

WHERE: 304 19th St. N, Bessemer

COST: Varies depending on selection

PRO TIP: Don't miss the signature dishes, like the Greek-style snapper or broiled seafood platter.

As a local, I'm drawn to the warm ambiance; the walls are adorned with photographs and memorabilia telling the story of Birmingham's past. The attentive staff, some of whom have been serving for decades, greet you like family, ensuring your experience is exceptional.

For visitors, the Bright Star offers a unique opportunity to savor authentic Southern flavors while soaking in the charm of a historic venue. The combination of delightful food, rich history, and welcoming service makes it a must-visit destination.

Whether you're celebrating a special occasion or indulging in a delicious meal, the Bright Star promises a memorable dining experience that showcases the best of Birmingham's culinary scene.

FIRST SCHOOL IN THE CITY

What school laid the foundation for the city's public education system?

Perched at the corner of 24th Street and Sixth Avenue, the Powell School stands as a monument to Birmingham's educational heritage. The school is named for James R. Powell, educator and Birmingham's first elected mayor. Although now vacant, the building echoes with the laughter and learning of the approximately 150 students who once filled its classrooms. This historic institution laid the foundation for the public school system in Birmingham, shaping the educational landscape for generations to come.

Powell School was founded in the late 19th century through a generous donation of land from the Elyton Land Company, demonstrating the community's commitment to education and progress. Its classrooms buzzed with the ambitions of young minds eager to learn, creating a vibrant atmosphere that fostered both academic and social development. Over the years, Powell School witnessed significant milestones in Birmingham's educational evolution. The school adapted to evolving educational practices, incorporating modern facilities and updated curricula to meet the changing needs of students. After surviving a fire in 2011, the building was preserved and repurposed, maintaining its historical significance while

POWELL SCHOOL

WHAT: Birmingham's first school

WHERE: Sixth Ave. N and 24th St.

COST: Free

PRO TIP: Although the Powell School is closed to visitors, it's still worth passing by for a walk or drive. You can admire the historical architecture from the outside and appreciate its significance as Birmingham's oldest surviving school building.

The Powell School is still standing, but it has been vacant for over two decades. Courtesy of Wally Argus

transforming into a modern residential and commercial space. It continued to serve as both a symbol of education and a cornerstone of community life.

For locals and educators alike, Powell School represents a crucial chapter in the story of Birmingham's public education. Its enduring presence reminds us of a time when education was the heartbeat of the community, a place where children gathered to learn not only academics but also the values of cooperation and citizenship.

As you walk past the building, you can almost feel the energy that once filled its halls—the excitement of new beginnings, the nurturing of dreams, and the forging of lifelong friendships. The Powell School is more than just bricks and mortar; it is a testament to the dedication and resilience of Birmingham's early educators and students. This site serves as a reminder of where it all began, inviting reflection on the journey of education in the Magic City.

The Powell School is Birmingham's oldest surviving school building and a significant piece of the city's history. Although closed to the public, the school's Romanesque Revival architecture and historical charm can still be admired from the outside.

FINEST ART COLLECTION IN THE SOUTHEAST

Where does art whisper its way into the everyday?

Art is alive, well, and on display in the Magic City. The Birmingham Museum of Art boasts one of the most extensive art collections in the Southeast. Situated in the heart of downtown Birmingham, it houses over 29,000 works of art from all across the globe. In addition to it's impressive collection, the museum stands out for its commitment to accessibility and inclusivity. Its efforts to make the experience inclusive to all visitors is different from most other museums.

Unlike traditional museums, The Birmingham Museum of Art offers a *Sensory Engaged Gallery*, where guests can interact with art through touch, sound, and movement. The museum also partners with KultureCity to provide sensory-friendly resources such as weighted lap pads, noise-canceling headphones, and sensory bags. Visitors with low to no vision can participate in specialized sensory tours that incorporate verbal descriptions and tactile

BIRMINGHAM MUSEUM OF ART

WHAT: A museum housing works of art from various cultures, including renowned collections of Asian, European, and American art

WHERE: 2000 Reverend Abraham Woods Jr. Blvd.

COST: Free

PRO TIP: Leave your big bags and purses behind. Smaller bags are recommended to keep from bumping the artwork.

The Birmingham Museum of Art showcases the city's thriving and diverse art scene. It is home to over 29,000 works spanning centuries and continents.

The Birmingham Museum of Art houses one of the most comprehensive American art collections in the south. Courtesy of Sean Pathasema

experiences, while those with color blindness can use EnChroma glasses to enhance their perception of artwork. This dedication to inclusivity makes the BMA not just a place to view art, but a space where everyone can engage with it in a meaningful way.

Founded in 1951, the Birmingham Museum of Art's diverse collection of paintings, sculptures, textiles, and decorative arts provides a captivating journey through time and cultures. Seasoned art lovers and curious explorers can spend hours enjoying all the museum has to offer.

One of the standout features in the museum is its impressive collection of Asian art, which is considered one of the best in the country. You will also find the acclaimed Kress Collection of Renaissance and Baroque paintings, making it a must-visit for those who appreciate European art history. But it's not just the global art scene that shines here—Southern regional art is also well-represented. In fact, visitors can catch a unique look at Alabama's artistic heritage.

Many visitors refer to the Birmingham Museum of Art as a peaceful retreat. It's a place where you can wander through galleries and discover something new each time you visit. In addition, the museum's sculpture garden, filled with lush greenery and striking works of art, offers a tranquil outdoor escape amid the city's hustle and bustle.

Visitors to Birmingham will find the museum to be a welcoming introduction to the city's rich cultural scene. Admission is free, making it an accessible and enriching experience for all. Whether you're exploring its internationally recognized exhibitions or simply enjoying a quiet afternoon among masterpieces, the Birmingham Museum of Art is an essential stop for anyone wanting to delve more deeply into the heart and soul of the Magic City.

1840S GREEK REVIVAL MANSION

Where can you see one of Birmingham's few surviving pre–Civil War structures?

What began as a modest four-room house built on 475 acres in the early 1800s had transformed into an eight-room mansion by 1850. Arlington Antebellum Home and Gardens, located near downtown Birmingham, is one of the city's few surviving Civil War–era structures. It was built with the labor of enslaved people whose names remain unknown but who are honored by a monument on the grounds. This mansion stands as a quiet reminder of Birmingham's deep historical roots.

This Greek Revival–style mansion once served as a headquarters for Union troops during the Civil War.

This beautifully preserved antebellum home offers a glimpse into 19th-century Birmingham. A visit to Arlington Antebellum Home and Gardens is a journey through history, charm, and timeless Southern hospitality.

ARLINGTON ANTEBELLUM HOME AND GARDENS

WHAT: Historical house and gardens

WHERE: 331 Cotton Ave. SW

COST: Admission prices vary. Group rates available for 10 or more people.

PRO TIP: After the tour, take some time to visit the peaceful gardens and capture some great photos.

Today, only six acres of the original estate remain. They have been preserved as they were when the mansion was built. It's one of the few opportunities visitors have to experience the natural beauty and architectural grace of the mid-19th century.

A tour of the Greek Revival mansion—now a museum and event center—begins with a journey through history. Guests are welcomed by stepping into a gift shop and sitting area where a short film gives an overview of the history of the home. As you explore the mansion and its gardens, you can't help but feel a sense of awe, knowing that this piece of history has stood the test of time, while Birmingham has grown up around it.

The historic importance of Arlington goes beyond its architectural beauty. It bears witness to both the antebellum South and the Civil Rights Movement, two critical pieces in the complex history of Birmingham's development.

Arlington Antebellum Home and Gardens offers visitors a serene experience. In addition to attracting visitors who want to tour the home and gardens, many historical, cultural, and civic activities take place at the mansion each year.

RESTING PLACE FOR BIRMINGHAM'S PIONEERS

What is one of the few places that was unsegregated, even during times of segregation in Birmingham?

Birmingham's first cemetery also holds another distinction: the first cemetery in Alabama to be placed on the National Register of Historic Places, inking its historical significance. Oak Hill Cemetery, located in North Birmingham, is the resting place for many pioneers of the Magic City.

Established in 1871 and designed by civil engineer Colonel William P. Barker, the cemetery was originally known as "City Cemetery," as noted by inscriptions on many of the original plats. Many notable Alabamians, from civil rights leader Fred Shuttlesworth to Sloss Furnaces founder James Sloss, are buried at Oak Hill Cemetery. You will also find the graves of Titanic survivor Philipp Mock and Alabama governor William Hugh Smith among the more than 11,000 burials inside the 21.5-acre cemetery.

Surprisingly, Oak Hill Cemetery was notably unsegregated, even during Birmingham's peak era of segregation. People of different races and backgrounds are buried together—a rare symbol of unity during a time of deep societal division.

You can almost feel a sense of community in the cemetery. The inscriptions on the stones contain dates and messages that

OAK HILL CEMETERY

WHAT: Birmingham's first and arguably most famous cemetery

WHERE: 1120 19th St. N

COST: Free self-guided tour. Fee for private guided tour.

PRO TIP: Wear comfortable shoes. The cemetery spans 21 acres and includes hilly terrain.

Oak Hill Cemetery, the city's oldest cemetery, preserves the stories of Birmingham's early settlers and many influential figures who shaped its growth.

tell stories. There's a son who fought bravely in the Civil War, a wife who brought laughter to her family, and a child whose life was ended much too soon. Many veterans from the Civil War, World War I, and World War II are buried at Oak Hill, too.

As visitors wander through the cemetery, the peaceful atmosphere is one of the first things they notice. Another thing that cannot be ignored is the remarkable collection of Victorian-era monuments and headstones in the cemetery. The intricate designs show the craftsmanship and artistic styles of the late 19th and early 20th centuries. Life-sized statues and intricate carvings will capture your attention and seem to watch you.

One of the most elaborate mausoleums in Oak Hill Cemetery belongs to Charles Linn, a prominent Birmingham financier. With bronze doors from Sweden, this grand structure sits on a hill where Linn requested to be buried, overlooking what he envisioned as the South's greatest industrial city.

Oak Hill Cemetery is not merely a collection of graves; it was a place where history breathed, inviting visitors to reflect on the past while appreciating the lives that contributed to Birmingham's vibrant legacy.

Local lore suggests that an unmarked grave in Oak Hill Cemetery is that of a women known only as "Aunt Jenny." She was a midwife who delivered hundreds of Birmingham's earliest residents, yet no official records of her full name exist.

LEGENDARY CAFETERIA LINE

What restaurant is known for its historic serving line?

Niki's West Steak & Seafood Restaurant is a staple of the Birmingham community. Since its opening in 1957, this cafeteria-style restaurant tucked away on Finley Avenue has been a go-to spot for locals looking for old-fashioned Southern food. Niki's West is over seven decades old, but it has maintained its charm and stayed true to its offerings of fresh meats, vegetables, and seafood. And, patrons have stayed true to Niki's West over the years.

NIKI'S WEST STEAK & SEAFOOD RESTAURANT

WHAT: Cafeteria-style restaurant

WHERE: 233 Finley Ave. W

COST: Refer to menu for current prices.

PRO TIP: The menu at Niki's West changes, so check the online menu ahead of time.

Niki's West is an experience. It's one of the few remaining cafeteria-style restaurants in the area. As you make your way down the legendary serving line, you'll have a difficult time choosing between the delicious Southern classics: collard greens, macaroni and cheese, fried chicken, catfish, and cornbread—to name a few. View the online menu ahead of time so you'll know which weekday to visit so you don't miss your favorites.

Niki's West is a cafeteria-style restaurant that serves delicious Southern classics. It has been a favorite of many Birmingham residents for nearly 70 years.

This cafeteria-style restaurant is known for its classic Southern dishes. Courtesy of Wally Argus

The atmosphere at Niki's West whispers a sense of history. Take some time to explore the black-and-white photos and memorabilia that tell stories of Birmingham's past. Natives and visitors alike will feel as if they've stepped into a page of Birmingham's story.

There's no shortage of Southern hospitality at Niki's West. It's one of those places where everyone knows you—and if they don't, they soon will. Once you pull up a chair, grab a plate, and savor the flavors, you'll see why Niki's West is one of Birmingham's treasures.

HEY, BATTER BATTER

How did black athletes participate in baseball during the era of segregation?

The history of baseball is incomplete without a mention of Birmingham. More specifically, it must include a mention of the Negro Southern League. The legacy of this league and its players is celebrated and preserved in the Negro Southern League Museum in downtown Birmingham.

The Negro Southern League was established in 1920 in response to segregation in organized baseball. The league provided a platform for black athletes to showcase their talents in a time when Major League Baseball remained out of reach for them. A visit to the Negro Southern League Museum will walk you through the history of black baseball and the legends that shaped a league that are still being honored over 100 years later.

From the moment you walk in, you are greeted with a rich collection of memorabilia that brings the greatness of this league to life. The Home Run Wall at the entrance immediately sets the tone and screams the magnitude of the black footprint in baseball history. Every artifact, from vintage uniforms to well-worn gloves and game programs, whispers stories of a past where determination met talent on dusty diamond fields.

As you walk through the museum, you're transported to a front-row seat behind home plate, cheering for legendary

---

The Negro Southern League Museum celebrates the untold stories of black baseball pioneers who shaped the sport's history. Through rare artifacts, interactive exhibits, and inspiring narratives, this museum captures the essence of Birmingham's baseball past.

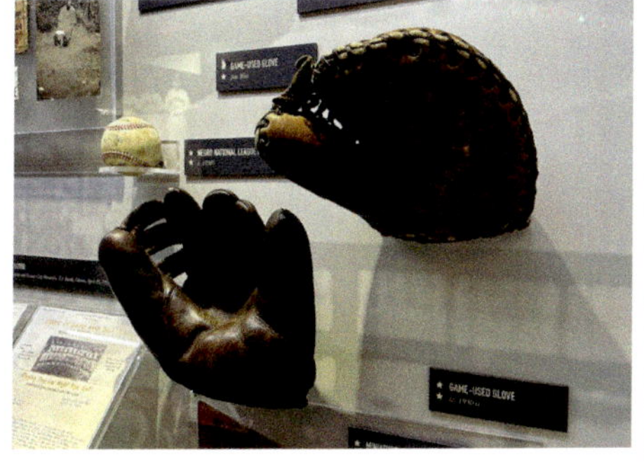

NEGRO SOUTHERN LEAGUE MUSEUM

WHAT: A museum that preserves the history of the Negro Southern League

WHERE: 120 16th St. S

COST: Free

PRO TIP: Right around the corner is Regions Field, where you'll discover a statue of Willie Mays.

players such as Leroy "Satchel" Paige, George "Mules" Suttles, and Willie Mays. These names, synonymous with greatness, are forever etched in baseball history. But the museum doesn't stop there—it celebrates modern-day legends who followed in their footsteps, like Michael Jordan, who famously spent a brief stint in baseball, and Bo Jackson, the Auburn phenom known for excelling in both football and baseball. Their inclusion serves as a reminder that the Negro Southern League's influence stretches far beyond its inception.

The museum doesn't just recount history; it honors the dreams that built it. It's a testament to how Birmingham played a vital role in both black baseball and civil rights, as these players broke barriers and pushed back against a segregated society. Visiting the Negro Southern League Museum is a journey into the heart of Birmingham's cultural and athletic legacy, one that continues to echo in the halls of the museum and across the city's ballfields today.

STATE-OF-THE-ART AUTO AND ENGINE MANUFACTURER

Where can you explore the facility responsible for producing all Honda light trucks globally?

If you drive a Honda Passport, Odyssey, Pilot, or Ridgeline, I bet you a dollar it was built near Birmingham. Wanna know why I'm so confident? The Alabama Auto Plant, just a stone's throw from the Magic City, is Honda's largest light truck production facility and the sole manufacturer of those vehicles.

Located in nearby Lincoln, this state-of-the-art plant not only churns out the rugged Ridgeline and versatile Odyssey but also produces the powerful V-6 engines that fuel them. With a workforce of over 4,500 employees, many of whom are proud Birmingham residents, this facility is a cornerstone of the local economy and a testament to the craftsmanship that defines the region.

What makes a visit to the Honda plant even more enticing? You can tour the facility and witness firsthand the incredible assembly process that brings your vehicle to life. Guided tours offer a behind-the-scenes look at

ALABAMA AUTO PLANT

WHAT: Honda manufacturing plant

WHERE: 1800 Honda Dr., Lincoln

COST: Free

PRO TIP: Check the website for information about tours.

Honda's Alabama Auto Plant is a cutting-edge facility where state-of-the-art robotics and advanced manufacturing techniques bring innovation to life.

Alabama Auto Plant is Honda's largest light truck production facility in the world. Courtesy of Alabama Auto Plant

the meticulous engineering and innovative technology that go into every Honda. You'll be amazed by the seamless blend of robotics and human skill.

But that's not all. Did you know that Honda has invested over $2 billion in Alabama since the plant's establishment in 2001? This commitment has not only transformed the landscape of automotive manufacturing in the region but also paved the way for numerous suppliers and support industries, creating thousands of jobs in and around Birmingham.

So, as you explore Birmingham, take a moment to appreciate the remarkable connection between this vibrant city and the vehicles that traverse its roads. It's a local story that's uniquely tied to the pulse of the community and the roar of the engines rolling off the assembly line.

FOLLOW THE GREEN TRAIL

What secret cascade lies so well hidden that you might need a ranger to point the way?

Just minutes south of Birmingham, you'll find Alabama's largest state park—Oak Mountain State Park. This expansive park offers over 9,900 acres of scenic natural beauty, which makes it a popular destination for outdoor enthusiasts. One of its most remarkable features is something you might not expect to find so close to an urban area—a beautiful waterfall tucked away in the woods. Known as Peavine Falls, this natural wonder is hidden deep within the park, so much so that park rangers say they frequently get requests from visitors asking for directions. Don't let that scare you away, though; the adventure is well worth it. Peavine Falls is an ideal spot to experience tranquility in the midst of nature.

PEAVINE FALLS

WHAT: Beautiful waterfall located in Oak Mountain State Park

WHERE: 200 Terrace Dr., Pelham

COST: A nominal admission fee required for entrance

PRO TIP: Wear sturdy, nonslip shoes if you plan to hike to the falls.

Several trails lead hikers to Peavine Falls, but the Green Trail is the most direct route. The Green Trail guides you through a forested area with diverse flora and fauna. Along

---

Peavine Falls is a stunning 65-foot waterfall that is perfect for hikers and nature lovers. A short hike rewards visitors with breathtaking views and a tranquil atmosphere.

This stunning waterfall is nestled in Oak Mountain State Park. It offers a serene escape from the bustle of the city. Courtesy of Wally Argus

the trail, you'll also enjoy magnificent views of towering trees and native plant life. While the Green Trail offers the quickest access, those seeking a more challenging or scenic route can choose from other trails that wind through different sections of the park. Each trail provides a unique perspective of the landscape.

The moderate to difficult trail ends with a reward: the serene beauty of Peavine Falls cascading down a rocky hillside. The base of the waterfall is a popular place for hikers to relax, snap photos, and appreciate the pristine environment. Experienced hikers and nature lovers agree that Peavine Falls is a hidden gem that showcases the unexpected beauty of Alabama's wilderness just outside Birmingham's city limits.

A WHISPER BENEATH THE WHISKEY

Could there really be a forgotten river beneath Birmingham—and a distillery on top of it?

A casual stop at a South Carolina distillery sparked a bold idea for Birmingham. During this casual visit among friends, orthopedic surgeon Dr. Jeff Dugas and former Auburn football player-turned-experimental marketer John Cubelic thought, "Why not bring a high-end craft distillery to the revitalized Magic City?" At the time, Birmingham had breweries, coffee roasters, and even craft popsicles. But not a single distillery.

So, the pair navigated the complexities of opening a legal distillery in Alabama. They visited more than 30 distilleries across the country to fine-tune their vision.

DREAD RIVER DISTILLING CO.

WHAT: Craft distillery offering small-batch spirits

WHERE: 2400 7th Ave. S

COST: Price varies based on selection.

PRO TIP: Take the distillery tour for a behind-the-scenes look at how their signature spirits are crafted.

The result? Dread River Distilling Co., a 24,000-square-foot spirits destination that opened quietly in 2019. It blends an industrial-chic aesthetic with a warm, sophisticated energy that feels equal parts cocktail lounge and secret lab.

Six months in, the pandemic brought everything to a halt. But instead of closing, Dread River shifted production to hand sanitizer, using its resources to serve the community. It was a move that showcased the grit and creativity that would later define the brand. When normal operations resumed, so did their mission of crafting exceptional bourbon, rye whiskey, vodka, gin, and other handcrafted spirits.

The Tuscan-inspired tasting room is the crown jewel: a stone-accented retreat with five luxe lounges, a main bar, and a private event space. Guests can sip cocktails, sample spirits, and enjoy food service. You can also tour the distillery.

And the name? Dread River is a nod to a mythical underground river said to flow beneath Birmingham, a hoax dreamed up by 19th-century storyteller Joseph Mulhatton. But the legend lives on.

Look closely at the interior design, and you'll spot tributes to Birmingham's industrial past: reclaimed wood, aged steel, and Prohibition-era details.

SUSTENANCE IN THE CITY

Where can you buy produce and local goods grown in and around the Magic City?

The farm-to-table concept has grown increasingly popular over the years. Birmingham makes it easy for residents to join in on the movement. Each Saturday, the Market at Pepper Place brings together local farmers, artisans, and food enthusiasts from up to 200 miles away, creating a true celebration of Alabama's rich agricultural heritage—all under the vision of a woman-owned business that's committed to uplifting the community.

This certified farmers market is open every Saturday from mid-January through mid-December, rain or shine, from 7 a.m. to 12 p.m. What's unique about this farmers market is that it hosts only vendors with Alabama-grown products. It's a place where friends run into each other, families start their weekends with fresh produce, and strangers bond over shared tastes and discoveries.

And you won't just find produce at the market. You can expect to find handmade crafts, artisan foods, and the sounds of live music filling the air. With roughly 80 vendors, Pepper Place is a feast for the senses. You'll see everything from seasonal fruits and vegetables to fresh bread, jams, and cheeses. Many of Birmingham's favorite chefs can often be spotted shopping here, gathering ingredients and inspiration for their next culinary masterpiece.

While at the market, grab a bite from local food vendors offering fresh, Southern-inspired dishes, or head to nearby spots like Post Office Pies for artisan pizza or Red Cat Coffee House for a coffee and pastry.

THE MARKET AT PEPPER PLACE

WHAT: A weekly farmers market

WHERE: 2829 Second Ave. S

COST: Free to browse, but bring money for produce and other goodies.

PRO TIP: Consider bringing reusable shopping bags with you.

You might stumble upon floral bundles designed to be burned like incense. Beautiful arrangements that release soothing scents as they smolder. Just steps away, you could find whimsical garden sculptures and rustic home décor crafted from reclaimed metal. It's that kind of unexpected creativity that makes the Market at Pepper Place feel full of hidden treasures waiting to be discovered.

Pepper Place Market, as it's often called, reports over 10,000 people in attendance during the height of the season, which reinforces its need in the community.

THE MINING YEARS

Where can you see remnants of Birmingham's mining past?

It's not so much of a secret that Birmingham has an impressive iron and steel history. In fact, buildings and statues scattered around the city hint at the immense impact of this industry on Birmingham's existence and growth. What might surprise you, though, is that there are remnants of Ruffner's mining years tucked away on Crusher Trail, hidden in plain sight on Ruffner Mountain.

As you hike along the Crusher Trail, you'll get an up-close look at an iron ore crusher—a massive piece of equipment used long ago to process the ore that helped build Birmingham. Rusted train tracks still wind through the area, where they once hauled heavy loads down the mountain. Along the path, you'll pass abandoned mine shafts, relics of a time when miners carved into Ruffner Mountain. These remnants serve as silent but powerful reminders of Birmingham's industrial past, creating a rare chance to step back into the city's gritty history while immersed in the beauty of the forest.

CRUSHER TRAIL

WHAT: Scenic recreation trail

WHERE: 1214 81st St. S

COST: Fee for parking pass

PRO TIP: Check Ruffner Mountain's website before you go—they sometimes offer guided hikes that dive more deeply into the history of the area.

After hiking Crusher Trail, check out Red Mountain Park and Sloss Furnaces to see old mining structures and learn more about Birmingham's history with iron-making.

Crusher Trail isn't just a journey into history; it's a true adventure for hikers. The path is rugged and offers a moderate-to-challenging climb, with rocky sections and steep inclines that make for an exhilarating hike. Along the way, you'll be rewarded with lush surroundings, towering trees, and a variety of wildlife—a surprising contrast to the heavy machinery and industrial relics that dot the landscape. As you reach higher points, you're treated to panoramic views of Birmingham's skyline peeking through the trees, a perfect blend of the city's modern-day pulse with its historic roots.

For locals and visitors alike, Crusher Trail is a hidden gem, offering a unique way to explore Birmingham's mining history while soaking in the natural beauty that now reclaims this storied mountain.

This old iron ore crusher once powered Birmingham's industrial boom.
Courtesy of Andre Natta

HAVEN FOR INJURED AND ORPHANED ANIMALS

Where do injured wildlife turn for care?

In 1977, Anne Miller and six dedicated volunteers founded the Alabama Wildlife Center (AWC), Alabama's oldest and largest wildlife rehabilitation facility. Over the past four decades, AWC has become a force in the conservation and care of native wildlife, annually treating thousands of injured or orphaned animals—primarily birds—with the goal of restoring them to the wild whenever possible.

Located in Oak Mountain State Park, the AWC offers a unique experience for visitors. Guests can explore the facility's educational exhibits to learn about Alabama's diverse wildlife and discover ways to safely and responsibly interact with wild animals. One of the highlights of visiting the center is the

This nonprofit center's focus is rehabilitating injured or orphaned wildlife and animals.

ALABAMA WILDLIFE CENTER

WHAT: Largest conservation organization in Alabama

WHERE: 100 Terrace Dr., Pelham

COST: Admission to the Alabama Wildlife Center is free, but there is an entrance fee to Oak Mountain State Park.

PRO TIP: Visit the Alabama Wildlife Center during feeding times to see rehabilitated birds of prey up close and learn about their recovery process from expert staff.

opportunity to observe some of the resident birds of prey, such as owls and hawks, which have injuries that prevent them from returning to the wild. These resident animals serve as ambassadors, helping the public understand the critical need for conservation efforts.

The AWC is committed to partnerships, working alongside local wildlife agencies and organizations to promote ethical standards in wild animal rehabilitation and care. Through these efforts, AWC aims not only to rehabilitate animals but also to inspire a lasting respect for Alabama's wildlife.

The Alabama Wildlife Center is the state's oldest and largest wildlife rehabilitation facility. Visitors can witness the incredible work of rescuing and rehabilitating birds while exploring nature.

CENTER FOR IRON AND STEEL PRODUCTION

What are the secret ingredients that give Birmingham its unique magic?

Within a 10-mile radius of Birmingham's city center, you'll find a natural abundance of coal, iron ore, and limestone—all the essential elements needed for iron production. This rare geological combination made Birmingham the ideal location for a thriving iron and steel industry, and it sparked an industrial boom that transformed the city into the "Magic City." Founded in 1871, Birmingham quickly became the South's leading industrial center, especially for iron and steel, fueling rapid economic growth and population expansion.

The city's growth drew people from all walks of life, including freed African Americans and poor white laborers from the rural South, all seeking new opportunities in the

THE MAGIC CITY

WHAT: Birmingham's legacy in reimagined buildings and spaces

WHERE: 200 19th St. N

COST: Admission fee to enter McWane Science Center

PRO TIP: Save plenty of time to admire and appreciate other reimagined spaces in the city.

booming industry. These laborers built and operated the mines, furnaces, and foundries that powered Birmingham's rise. Many settled in newly formed neighborhoods surrounding the factories, further accelerating the city's growth.

Today, Birmingham's skyline and neighborhoods still reflect its industrial past. Old factories and warehouses have been repurposed into modern lofts, galleries, and unique spaces that merge the city's history with contemporary urban life. Iconic structures like Sloss Furnaces—a former iron-producing blast furnace—offer visitors a look into Birmingham's industrial legacy.

As you explore the city, take a moment to appreciate the natural resources and historic structures that have shaped Birmingham's identity.

Birmingham's industrial past lives on through repurposed spaces like Railroad Park, once a vacant lot and now the city's "front yard," and the historic Loveman's of Alabama building, now home to the McWane Science Center.

Birmingham quickly became an industrial powerhouse due to its abundance of natural resources—coal, iron ore, and limestone. Courtesy of Richard Melanson

THANKS FOR THE MEMORIES

THE MUSEUM OF FOND MEMORIES AT REED BOOKS

WHAT: An eclectic blend of rare books and nostalgic memorabilia

WHERE: 2021 Third Ave. N

COST: Free to visit

PRO TIP: Make sure to give yourself plenty of time to browse.

Where can you find both rare books and items that spark moments of nostalgia?

Inside a building in downtown Birmingham marked "Antiques-Books-Collectibles," you'll find the Museum of Fond Memories at Reed Books—a two-in-one gem where you can grab titles that you've always wanted and obscure items that you didn't even know you needed. This must-see spot is the creation of Jim Reed, a passionate collector and storyteller who has spent decades curating this unique space.

At first glance, you might be overwhelmed by the organized randomness that's been collecting in the store since 1980. But a closer look might turn into hours of examining unique and rare items that you're not likely to see anywhere else, many of which are available for purchase.

In addition to books, you can find anything from stickers and toys to albums and other

You could easily spend hours exploring this whimsical collection of rare books, vintage treasures, and nostalgic wonders—and don't forget to meet the owner, Jim Reed.

whimsical treasures. I challenge you to walk through the store without experiencing a moment of nostalgia.

Every piece of quirky memorabilia in the store tells a story. The interactive displays capture your attention and prompt you to share your own fond memories. Thankfully, Reed stands ready to hear your story and share a few of his own.

Jim Reed has created a one-of-a-kind store that blends a bookstore with a nostalgia-filled museum. It's easy to lose track of time exploring its treasures.

BOUTIQUE BED & BREAKFAST

Where can you find a cozy getaway nestled in nature?

If you're looking for a bit of tranquility that's not too far from the city, take a short drive to Buck Creek BnB. This hidden gem is the retreat you've been looking for. In the heart of Helena, and just down the road from Birmingham, you'll be surrounded by serene natural beauty and the peaceful sound of flowing water.

BUCK CREEK BNB

WHAT: A boutique bed-and-breakfast and spa

WHERE: 49 Lake Davidson Ln., Helena

COST: Check website for pricing details.

PRO TIP: Plan to spend some time exploring the nearby Buck Creek trails and the charming shops in Old Town Helena.

At Buck Creek BnB, no detail is overlooked. The elegant rooms are inviting and comfortable and designed with the right mix of elegant decor and cozy touches that make you feel right at home. And the views? Simply stunning—many rooms overlook the creek, where the sound of flowing water invites you to unwind.

It's worth mentioning the "A Massage Two Remember" package, which brings the spa experience to you with in-room therapeutic massages designed to melt the stress away. They offer a variety of packages that are perfect for a solo self-care day, a girls' weekend, or any other special occasion.

Buck Creek BnB is surrounded by scenic hiking trails that are perfect for exploring the natural beauty of the area.

The serenity of Buck Creek BnB is just a short drive from Birmingham. Courtesy of Buck Creek BnB

Even though you're tucked away from the hustle and bustle, you're still surrounded by quaint local shops, scenic trails, and quick access to everything Birmingham has to offer. It's the perfect spot for those looking for a moment of respite.

ONCE-TALLEST SKYSCRAPER IN THE CITY

Where can you find a building that still holds secrets from its banking past?

One of the most recognizable signs in Birmingham is the vintage red neon "City Federal" sign, which has illuminated the skyline for decades. Ask a local 30-something about this building, and they'll likely describe it as a high-rise of luxury condos. But if you speak to someone who's been around a bit longer, they'll remember it as the original home of the City Federal Savings and Loan Association.

This 27-story building has been a local icon since its completion in 1913. Once the tallest building in the Southeast, City Federal held that title for over half a century and remains one of the tallest buildings in Alabama today. In 1984, it was added to the National Register of Historic Places, a testament to its architectural significance and its important place in the city's history.

Beyond its panoramic views, City Federal has always held an air of mystery. A chat with some current residents reveals stories about abandoned rooms and vaults from the building's days as a financial institution, supposedly sealed off and untouched for decades. There's speculation about what these

---

The City Federal Building was designed by William Weston, a renowned architect behind many of Birmingham's most notable buildings like the Woodward Building, the Frank Nelson Building, and the Brown Marx Building.

spaces might contain—perhaps records, artifacts, or relics of a bygone era—adding to the building's allure and mystique.

That sense of mystery hasn't stopped people from flocking to the top floors, where the building remains a popular venue for events. Whether it's for a wedding, an anniversary celebration, or even a memorable proposal, the panoramic views and timeless charm of City Federal continue to make it one of the most coveted spots to celebrate life's special moments in the Magic City.

CITY FEDERAL BUILDING

WHAT: A historic 27-story skyscraper that was once the tallest building in the city

WHERE: 2024 Second Ave. N

COST: Free

PRO TIP: The City Federal Building boasts some of the best vantage points in the city, but access is limited to those who live there—or know a resident.

With its iconic neon sign still lighting up Birmingham's skyline, City Federal isn't just a building—it's a symbol of the city's growth, history, and enduring allure.

This building is a symbol of Birmingham's rich history. Courtesy of James Willamor

FAST LANE FANTASY

Where can you learn to drive like the pros?

There is only one place in the United States where you can attend the official US driving school of Porsche. That place is located just outside Birmingham.

This lesser-known treasure for high-performance car enthusiasts is located inside Barber Motorsports Park. This experience is more than a driving school—it's an adrenaline-fueled adventure that merges precision engineering with high-performance training.

The Porsche Track Experience offers a variety of programs tailored to different skill levels and goals, from single-day introductory courses to multi-day sessions designed to sharpen the skills of advanced drivers. Professional instructors guide participants through techniques for cornering, accelerating, and braking, offering insights that deepen participants' appreciation of what a Porsche can do on a high-caliber course. This individualized coaching, often held on Barber's 2.38-mile, 16-turn track, makes the experience as informative as it is thrilling.

PORSCHE TRACK EXPERIENCE

WHAT: A world-class driving school at Barber Motorsports Park

WHERE: 6075-B Barber Motorsports Pkwy., Leeds

COST: Varies

PRO TIP: Entry-level courses can be booked online. The best time to visit is on weekdays, when the track is less crowded.

At the Porsche Track Experience in Birmingham, you don't have to own a Porsche or have racing experience to participate.

Courtesy of Porsche Track Experience

What makes this place extra special is its peaceful, almost secret location within Barber Motorsports Park. Surrounded by the green, manicured landscapes and artful sculptures that dot the park, it's an unexpected setting for such an exhilarating experience. Participants—ranging from Porsche enthusiasts to corporate teams looking for a unique retreat—come from across the country to experience a program that's immersive and exciting.

With such a rare opportunity so close to Birmingham, the Porsche Track Experience at Barber Motorsports Park remains a must-discover for anyone who has a passion for driving, an admiration for Porsche, or simply a need for speed.

TELL ME A STORY

Are you ready to discover the hidden talents of the Storyteller Fountain?

Birmingham is full of quirky landmarks, and the Storyteller Fountain in Five Points South is a prime example. This whimsical yet controversial fountain was commissioned as a tribute to Malcolm McRae, a beloved art dealer who died tragically. McRae's mother wanted a lively, public space that captured Birmingham's spirit, and so the Storyteller Fountain was born.

The sculpture, created by artist Frank Fleming, depicts an eccentric collection of fairytale creatures gathered around a central ram, evoking the image of a peaceful kingdom. The design is open to interpretation, but this freedom has also sparked controversy. While some admire the fountain's enchanting charm, others see darker undertones, dubbing it "The Satanic Fountain" due to its unusual characters and design. These rumors only add to its mystique, sparking curiosity among locals and visitors alike.

Since its unveiling in 1992, the Storyteller Fountain has become a beloved landmark. Despite the initial controversy, the

---

The Storyteller Fountain is one of the most controversial sculptures in the city. Its whimsical and unconventional design frequently sparks conversation among residents.

This unique work of art sits in Five Points South and is a conversation piece for locals and visitors alike.

STORYTELLER FOUNTAIN

WHAT: A unique bronze sculpture located in Five Points South

WHERE: 1001 20th St. S

COST: Free

PRO TIP: The Storyteller Fountain is close to landmarks like the Brother Bryan Statue and Vulcan Park Museum. Many local restaurants are also nearby.

fountain has firmly established itself as part of Birmingham's unique character. It's undergone maintenance and preservation efforts over the years, and its fairytale figures and mysterious aura remain intact for future generations to enjoy.

No matter whether you see it as a simple piece of whimsical art or something more mysterious, the Storyteller Fountain is a fascinating part of Birmingham's story—a place where fantasy meets reality, and every visitor can create their own interpretation of its meaning.

TREEHOUSE FULL OF BOOKS

Where can you read a book and then hike a trail?

You might wonder how a library ended up in a book about secrets in Birmingham. Libraries are public spaces, after all, but the Vestavia Hills Library in the Forest is no ordinary library—it's a community treasure. Known for its seamless blend of literature and environmental stewardship, it's the first library in Alabama to achieve a LEED (Leadership in Energy and Environmental Design) Gold certification. This green design focus goes beyond appearances: over 80 percent of the wood harvested during its construction was repurposed for its furnishings and interiors. This characteristic creates a sense of natural unity between the library and the surrounding forest.

VHLF offers more than just shelves of books. It also features a maker space complete with 3D printers, vinyl cutters, a photography studio, and a range of tools for hands-on creativity. Visitors will also find a unique selection of items to check out, including hammocks, cognitive care kits, and even walking sticks, perfect for exploring the library's trail, which features a bridge and a waterfall.

In addition, the Vestavia Hills Library in the Forest offers a full calendar of events tailored to all ages. From children's story times and teen workshops to book clubs, art classes, and adult activities, there's something for everyone. The library

---

The Vestavia Hills Library in the Forest is an ergonomic space that offers expansive reading spaces, state-of-the-art technology, and scenic views.

frequently hosts seasonal events and educational programs that connect community members with local experts and artists. VHLF is truly a space for learning and community engagement.

From its eco-conscious design to its unique resources and amenities, the Vestavia Hills Library in the Forest offers an immersive experience unlike any other library in the area. It's a peaceful retreat that combines community, nature, and innovation.

VESTAVIA HILLS LIBRARY IN THE FOREST

WHAT: Alabama's first LEED-certified library

WHERE: 1221 Montgomery Hwy., Vestavia Hills

COST: Free

PRO TIP: Pack your sneakers. After enjoying a good book, take a relaxing walk on the library's scenic trail to enjoy the peaceful surroundings.

Courtesy of Vestavia Hills Library in the Forest

WHERE WATER MEETS HISTORY

Where can you find one of Birmingham's first waterworks facilities?

Birmingham's original water pumping station sits on the edge of the Cahaba River and is one of the city's best-kept secrets. The Cahaba Pumping Station, built in 1887, was once the heartbeat of the city's water supply. It now stands as a working museum and event center. The station was designed by Elyton Land Company engineer Willis Milner.

What makes the Cahaba Pumping Station different from other industrial buildings of its time is its stunning architectural details. It showcases towering arches, intricate decorative tiles, and beautiful stained glass windows, which make it a rare example of a pumping station with such aesthetic elegance. The building's design reflects the industrial sophistication of the late 19th century by incorporating both form and function in a way that is seldom seen in similar structures.

Inside the museum, visitors can explore the original control rooms, boiler houses, and pump houses that have

CAHABA PUMPING STATION MUSEUM

WHAT: A historic water-pumping station

WHERE: 4012 Sicard Hollow Rd.

COST: Free

PRO TIP: The business hours are posted on the website, but it's a good idea to call before your visit to make sure someone will be there.

The Cahaba Pumping Station is one of the city's earliest waterworks facilities.

This iconic piece of Birmingham's waterworks history still serves the city today. Courtesy of Tim Carr

been meticulously preserved. The preservation of these spaces is a testament to the station's historical significance. In 1988, the building underwent a major renovation that earned it a Preservation Award from the Birmingham Historical Society.

In addition to being a museum, the Cahaba Pumping Station functions as a venue for educational programs, community events, and civic gatherings.

SPIRITS IN THE MAGIC CITY

Have you ever wondered where Birmingham's smoothest spirits are crafted?

NBA legend Charles Barkley is known for his basketball skills and his larger-than-life personality. More recently, he's made a name for himself as majority owner of an award-winning distilling company tucked in Birmingham's Lakeview district. Barkley has helped position Redmont Distilling Co. as a leader for Southern spirits. This 10-year-old distillery has earned accolades like "Best Vodka in the US" at the prestigious San Francisco World Spirits Competition. It also has the distinction of being the first legal, licensed distillery in Birmingham since Prohibition.

But Redmont isn't just about the awards and distinctions—it's about innovation and authenticity. The distillery takes pride in its clean-label ethos. Redmont Vodka is gluten-free and distilled multiple times to achieve a crisp, smooth finish. And while vodka is their flagship, whispers among insiders often point to the distillery's experiments with aged spirits—think small-batch bourbons that haven't yet hit the shelves but are quietly redefining Alabama's whiskey game.

What many don't know is how deep Redmont's ties to the community run. Behind the scenes, the company actively collaborates with local farmers, sourcing ingredients that keep its products firmly rooted in Alabama. Barkley himself is

---

At Redmont Distilling, Southern spirits are steeped in tradition but distilled with a modern twist—it's where the old meets the bold.

known to drop by the distillery unannounced, chatting with staff and customers alike, sharing his vision for making Redmont not just a brand but a Birmingham institution.

For Barkley, who grew up just down the road in Leeds, Redmont is a homecoming of sorts—a chance to invest in the community that shaped him. "It's not just about the vodka," he's fond of saying. "It's about building something special, something we can all be proud of."

REDMONT DISTILLING CO

WHAT: A craft distillery specializing in premium spirits, particularly vodka and whiskey

WHERE: 4550 Fifth Ave. S, Building N

COST: Varies

PRO TIP: For a unique experience, consider visiting one of the local bars or restaurants that features Redmont Distilling's spirits in their cocktails.

LONGEST-SURVIVING GREEK-OWNED HOT DOG STAND

What draws people back to this place time and time again?

Birmingham's food and restaurant story cannot be told without including a mention of Gus's Hot Dogs, the city's longest-surviving Greek-owned hot dog stand. Greek immigrant Gus Alexander opened Gus's Hot Dogs in 1947, and the Fourth Avenue North restaurant still operates today in the same location. Over the years, it has become more than just a place to grab a tasty hot dog; it's another entry in the Magic City's rich heritage of Greek-owned eateries.

Over the decades, Gus's has passed through several hands, and each owner has added to its legacy. After Gus sold the business in the 1960s, it was carried forward by Aleck Choraitis and later George Nasiakos. Today, Lee Pantazis continues the tradition, crafting high-quality, affordable hot dogs that have become iconic in Birmingham's food scene.

The standout menu item, the "Special Dog," is a feast of flavors: a grilled hot dog nestled in a steamed bun, topped with mustard, onions, sauerkraut, ground beef, and secret sauce. According to Pantazis, this combination is a holdover from when Greek-owned hot dog purveyors added extra meat for extra sustenance for the hard-working industry folks of Birmingham.

GUS'S HOT DOGS

WHAT: An eatery downtown known for its classic, no-frills approach to serving hot dogs

WHERE: 1915 Fourth Ave. N

COST: Prices vary.

PRO TIP: Go during off-peak hours to avoid the lunch rush, and make sure to try the signature "Special Sauce" for the full Gus's experience.

Gus's Hot Dogs is a local favorite that's been satisfying cravings for generations.

Pair the Special Dog with a Grapico soda and a bag of Golden Flake chips, and you've got a meal steeped in Southern nostalgia.

Beyond the food, Gus's is a symbol of community and continuity. It's a place where families have shared meals for generations, where memories are tied as much to the food as to the friendly service and vibrant downtown location. A hidden gem inside this modest building is a tiny walk-in vault. It's a relic from when the space operated as a bank. Now repurposed as a storage area, most customers overlook it, but it offers a surprising glimpse into Birmingham's past, tucked away in a no-frills hot dog joint. Even as the city evolves, Gus's remains a cherished constant, connecting Birmingham residents to a simpler, tastier past.

Gus's has gained a reputation beyond the local scene. Over the years, it's been mentioned in several food blogs, TV shows, and even movies as a must-try spot in town!

A TRIBUTE TO BIRMINGHAM'S CULINARY ICON

Where can you sit at the table honoring one of Birmingham's most renowned chefs?

Frank Stitt is widely known as one of Birmingham's culinary icons, celebrated for his profound influence on the city's food culture. To honor his contributions, a sculpture was created at the 24th Street entrance of Birmingham's Rotary Trail. This distinctive piece, a stainless steel, marble, and glass table surrounded by chairs, stands as a testament to Stitt's legacy and the power of community.

Designed by artist Greg Fitzpatrick, the sculpture was commissioned as part of the Alabama-Mississippi Chapter of the National Multiple Sclerosis Society's Legacy of Leadership program. Fitzpatrick's design embodies a theme close to Stitt's heart, which is using food to bring people together. The table, with its sleek yet inviting design, symbolizes Stitt's commitment to fostering connection and belonging through shared meals and vibrant culinary experiences.

FRANK'S TABLE

WHAT: Sculpture honoring Birmingham chef Frank Stitt

WHERE: 24th St. S and First Ave. S

COST: Free

PRO TIP: Take a moment to explore the surrounding Rotary Trail after visiting the sculpture.

Unveiled in November 2019, the sculpture not only honors Stitt's career but also highlights Birmingham's rise as a culinary destination under his influence. His restaurants Chez Fonfon, Bottega, and the James Beard Award-winning Highlands Bar & Grill (now closed) have long been landmarks of Southern

Frank's Table *is a tribute to one of Birmingham's most iconic chefs and restaurateurs.*

cuisine with a French flair, drawing national attention to the city's food scene.

More than just a tribute, *Frank's Table* is a gathering place, inviting locals and visitors alike to pause, reflect, and celebrate the shared joy of food. It serves as a reminder of how Stitt's vision has transformed Birmingham into a destination where food is more than sustenance—it's a cultural connection.

Frank's Table symbolizes community, culinary excellence, and Frank Stitt's lasting impact on Birmingham's dining scene.

A STROLL THROUGH ARTISTIC MASTERPIECES

Where else can you admire artwork while standing inside a masterpiece?

The Abroms-Engel Institute for the Visual Arts (AEIVA) is one of Birmingham's hidden art treasures. It offers a distinctive blend of contemporary art exhibitions, cultural enrichment, and community engagement. The institute opened in 2014 and has quickly become a favorite for both local and international artists. Located on the University of Alabama at Birmingham (UAB) campus, AEIVA is open to students and the broader Birmingham community.

AEIVA's exhibitions span from traditional visual arts to cutting-edge contemporary works. It plays a pivotal role in supporting emerging talent through its annual Bachelor of Fine Arts exhibition, which showcases the work of UAB's graduating students each spring. This commitment to nurturing the next generation of artists sets AEIVA apart and ensures the continual evolution of Birmingham's art scene.

ABROMS-ENGEL INSTITUTE FOR THE VISUAL ARTS AT UAB

WHAT: Contemporary arts institution

WHERE: 1221 10th Ave. S

COST: Free

PRO TIP: Plan your visit during exhibition openings or special events.

AEIVA is one of the many places you can explore Birmingham's growing arts scene.

AEIVA is a vital part of Birmingham's thriving art scene. Courtesy of Wally Argus

The art doesn't just live on the inside. The building itself, designed by the renowned architect Randall Stout, is a work of art. The 26,000-square-foot space, funded by lead donors Judy and Hal Abroms and Ruth and Marvin Engel, features sleek, modern architecture that draws visitors in from the moment they arrive. With six to nine rotating exhibits each year, AEIVA offers a space for not only visual art but also performances, lectures, and artist talks. The institute also houses academic classrooms and faculty offices, solidifying its role as an educational resource for UAB students and faculty.

If you're an art aficionado or simply curious about the cultural pulse of Birmingham, plan a visit to AEIVA.

SCRAP-IRON STORY OF CULTURE AND HERITAGE

How can objects tell powerful stories about slavery, civil rights, and the African diaspora?

Joe Minter's African Village in America is a unique outdoor art environment located near Birmingham's historic Elmwood Cemetery. This compelling site, built on Minter's property, is a testament to African American history and culture. The village combines sculpture, storytelling, and symbolism. For over 30 years, Minter has transformed his backyard into a spiritual and cultural landmark, drawing visitors from around the world.

The village is a living, evolving installation, with objects like tools, toys, and discarded materials meticulously repurposed to reflect themes of slavery, civil rights, and African heritage. Minter's work is deeply personal and conveys messages of justice, resilience, and faith. The installations also include commentary on global issues and tributes to historical events like the Birmingham civil rights movement.

Minter's work has gained international attention, being featured in exhibits at the Metropolitan Museum of Art and the Smithsonian National Museum of African American History and Culture. Despite this recognition, the village remains an intimate, grassroots creation, staying true to Minter's vision of educating and inspiring visitors.

JOE MINTER'S AFRICAN VILLAGE IN AMERICA

WHAT: Outdoor art exhibit focusing on African American history and culture

WHERE: 931 Nassau Ave. SW

COST: Free

PRO TIP: The site is located on private property, and tours are often guided by Joe Minter himself for a more personal experience.

Joe Minter is the mastermind behind this ever-evolving display of art located on the southwest edge of Birmingham. Courtesy of Kelly Ludwig

What sets the African Village apart is its immersive and emotional experience. Visitors often describe feeling a deep connection to the stories embedded in the sculptures. Minter himself often greets guests and offers personal insights into his creations. It's a must-see for those exploring Birmingham's lesser-known cultural gems.

Joe Minter's African Village in America is a thought-provoking outdoor museum made entirely from found objects. This powerful installation honors African American history.

BISTRO IN BIRMINGHAM

Where can you dine in a cozy café in the city?

When you step into Chez Fonfon, located in Birmingham's Southside, you'll feel as if you've been transported straight to a Parisian bistro. The intimate, cozy atmosphere welcomes you with its warm, rustic decor—dark wood, vintage French posters, and soft lighting. The restaurant's modest exterior offers little hint of the refined culinary experience that lies within. Over the years, the restaurant has quietly cultivated a devoted following among those who know where to look. For first-time guests, the contrast between the casual, bistro-style atmosphere and the expertly crafted dishes often comes as a delightful surprise. It's a reminder that world-class dining doesn't always announce itself, but rather reveals itself through intention, tradition, and quiet excellence. Founded by Frank Stitt, one of Birmingham's culinary icons, Chez Fonfon serves up authentic French fare with a Southern twist. The menu offers classics like coq au vin, steak frites, and

CHEZ FONFON

WHAT: French café located in Birmingham's Five Points South

WHERE: 2007 11th Ave. S

COST: Varies depending on selection

PRO TIP: Make a reservation, especially if you're planning to visit during peak hours or on weekends.

You don't have to hop a plane for a refined dining experience in the city. At Chez Fonfon, you can experience dishes like escargot, steak frites, and moules marinières.

Indulge in French cuisine with a Birmingham flair at Chez Fonfon. Credit Wally Argus

French onion soup, all meticulously prepared to showcase Stitt's renowned culinary artistry.

Chez Fonfon sets the bar high with its attention to detail. The dishes are crafted with local, seasonal ingredients, elevating traditional French flavors with the finest offerings from Alabama's farmers and purveyors. Stitt's influence on Birmingham's food scene is undeniable, and Chez Fonfon is a testament to his mastery and commitment to the art of dining.

This restaurant is perfect for enjoying a romantic dinner or gathering with friends. It offers a timeless dining experience, where you can indulge in exquisite food.

Chez Fonfon stands as a staple in Birmingham's ever-growing culinary landscape. Every visit feels like a celebration of the city's rich food culture and Stitt's legacy. It's a place where both locals and visitors come to savor not just a meal, but an experience.

BLOOMING BOOKS AND BLOSSOMS

Where can you find the only horticultural library in the area?

Jefferson County boasts over 40 libraries as part of its "one county–one library card" system, but the Library at the Birmingham Botanical Gardens is truly something special. As one of the few public horticultural libraries in the United States, it offers an extensive collection of resources aimed at making plants and gardening accessible to all.

Tucked away inside the Garden Center, the library can be easy to miss if you're not looking for the signs. But don't

The library at the Birmingham Botanical Garden is the only horticultural library in the area.

The Library at the Gardens offers more than just horticultural resources—it's full of unique features. After strolling through the gardens, stop by the library to learn more about the plants and sights you encountered along the way.

BIRMINGHAM BOTANICAL GARDENS LIBRARY

WHAT: Library located at Birmingham Botanical Gardens

WHERE: 2612 Lane Park Rd.

COST: Free

PRO TIP: Check out the rotating schedule of events and workshops.

let its small size fool you. The library is packed with over 14,000 books, DVDs, audiobooks, and magazines. It's a full-service library with a broad selection of gardening materials, indoor and outdoor seating, and even a children's section.

In addition to gardening books, you'll find resource materials for the Hands-On Activities Science Program, multiple copies of Peterson First Guides, and the entire Emmy-winning *Discovering Alabama* series on DVD. Plus, if you need more materials, you can access resources from any of the other 39 libraries in the Jefferson County Library Cooperative.

Some other unique features of the library include a large selection of gardening resources, a free seed exchange, a teacher resource center, and a local art gallery.

As a program of the Friends of Birmingham Botanical Gardens, the library is committed to environmental education, connecting the community with nature, and nurturing a passion for plants. It empowers visitors to carry the gardens' mission beyond its grounds and encourages lifelong learning about the environment.

DIRIGIBLE LANDING POST

Where can an airship land in Birmingham?

Perched on the top of the Thomas Jefferson Tower is a quirky piece of history: its zeppelin mooring mast. This structure was an original part of the luxurious Thomas Jefferson Hotel and was designed to be a beacon for airships. Imagine that—dirigibles docking right on top of a downtown hotel!

ZEPPELIN MOORING MAST

WHAT: Mooring mast atop the Thomas Jefferson Tower

WHERE: 1623 Second Ave. N

COST: Free

PRO TIP: Access to the top of the Thomas Jefferson Tower is typically restricted. Keep an eye on local events or reach out to the building management for opportunities to explore this historical feature.

The idea was ahead of its time, and sadly, the mooring mast was never actually used. Interestingly, the mooring mast was said to be a part of a clever publicity stunt. The story says the hotel's management decided to capitalize on the public's fascination with airships by promoting the idea of dirigibles docking at the hotel. The stunt generated significant buzz and drew attention to the hotel.

After the Hindenburg disaster in 1937, the popularity of airships plummeted, and the mast was removed in 1950. Fast forward to 2017, and the mast made a surprising reappearance during the tower's restoration. Now, it stands as an iconic

---

In addition to Birmingham, cities like New York City, Chicago, and Los Angeles were said to be a part of the dirigible mooring mast publicity stunt.

Above: *This timeless Birmingham landmark stands tall, reflecting the city's rich history and evolving skyline. Courtesy SPmedit*

Left: *Atop the Thomas Jefferson Tower is perched a large mast intended for mooring airships—but it has never been used.*

reminder of Birmingham's bold ambitions and its ever-evolving skyline. It serves as a unique conversation piece for residents and visitors alike.

The removal and replacement of the mast aligns with the journey of the tower itself, which has seen quite a transformation.

RAINY DAY REVOLUTION

Did you know the woman who invented windshield wipers was from Birmingham?

Next time you're driving through a rainstorm and your windshield wipers spring into action, take a moment to consider this: The woman who invented the windshield wiper was from Birmingham. Mary Anderson, a visionary well ahead of her time, gifted the world a practical innovation that continues to make our commutes safer and more comfortable today.

In 1902, while visiting New York City, Anderson witnessed a scene that would forever alter the course of driving history. She observed streetcar drivers struggling to maintain visibility during rainstorms, either leaning out the window or relying on an assistant to manually wipe the windshield. Not only was this method inefficient and impractical, it was also dangerous.

This observation sparked an idea. What if there were a way to clear the windshield without requiring the driver to leave their seat? Anderson devised a mechanical solution: a spring-loaded arm with a rubber blade, which could be controlled from within the vehicle. In 1903, she patented the design, which laid the groundwork for what would become the modern windshield wiper.

Unfortunately, Anderson did not see significant financial reward from her invention during her lifetime. In fact, it

---

Mary Anderson's invention of the windshield wiper in 1903 revolutionized driving. Although her patent was initially met with resistance, her innovation became a standard feature in vehicles, cementing her place in history as a trailblazer in automotive technology.

Mary Anderson, the inventor of the windshield wiper, has ties to Birmingham.

INVENTION OF WINDSHIELD WIPERS

WHAT: Mary Anderson is buried at Elmwood Cemetery.

WHERE: 600 Martin Luther King Jr. Dr.

COST: Free

PRO TIP: Stop by the Elmwood Cemetery office for a map of notable gravesites.

wasn't until decades later, when cars became more widespread and safety concerns grew, that her design was truly embraced.

Nonetheless, Anderson's ingenuity has endured. So, the next time you're behind the wheel in a downpour, remember that this simple yet groundbreaking invention—born right here in the Magic City—changed the way we drive.

CAFÉ WITH A SIDE OF QUIRK

Where can you have lunch at a café that served as the inspiration for a movie setting?

The Irondale Cafe is known for its Southern comfort food. While the fried chicken and fried green tomatoes often steal the spotlight, there are a few other things that make this unassuming restaurant stand out.

One of the most fascinating aspects of the Irondale Cafe is its role in the making of Fried Green Tomatoes—the film that cemented the café's place in pop culture. Though the movie's fictional Whistle Stop Cafe was not filmed here, the Irondale Cafe was the inspiration for the setting. During filming, the café became a hangout spot for the cast and crew, adding a touch of Hollywood magic to this small-town restaurant.

The building itself also carries its own history. Originally a railroad depot, it served as a transportation hub before transitioning into a local dining spot. Its roots in the town's early days give the café a distinct character and connection to Birmingham's past.

What truly sets the Irondale Cafe apart is the fact that it has been owned by the same family for over 30 years. That personal, family-run touch gives the restaurant a warmth and authenticity that makes it feel like home.

IRONDALE CAFE

WHAT: Historic café in Irondale

WHERE: 1906 First Ave. N

COST: Refer to menu for current prices.

PRO TIP: Save a bit of time to visit the train observation deck right across the street from the Irondale Cafe. Arrive early to avoid the lunch rush, and make sure to try the fried green tomatoes.

This cafe was made famous by the film Fried Green Tomatoes, *which also happens to be the cafe's most famous menu item.*

And of course, we can't forget the fried green tomatoes, a must-try at the Irondale Cafe. It's said that they serve between 600 and 800 slices each day, a testament to their popularity with diners.

The Irondale Cafe is more than just a place for good food; it's a beloved piece of Birmingham's history, filled with quirky charm and a rich story to tell.

The movie *Fried Green Tomatoes* put Irondale Cafe on the map, but locals will argue it's been a favorite for many years.

LIGHTS, CAMERA, BIRMINGHAM!

Where can you watch an independent film in Birmingham?

If you love good movies and a good time, you might want to check out the Sidewalk Film Center + Cinema, located in the historic Pizitz Building in downtown Birmingham. This two-screen cinema is more than just a place to catch a flick—it's a spot where indie films, documentaries, and unique stories come to life in a space that feels like it was made for movie lovers.

As soon as you step inside, you're greeted by a sleek, modern vibe that makes you want to settle in and stay awhile. The lobby has a café bar serving drinks and snacks, while the walls showcase posters from past films shown at the Sidewalk Film Festival. And speaking of the festival—this place is the heart of the annual event, which has been lighting up the city since 1999. The festival is a huge deal that draws filmmakers and film buffs from all over the world.

The Sidewalk Film Center + Cinema offers cozy theaters and a chic café bar, making it the ideal spot to enjoy indie films, dive into film culture, and connect with a lively creative community. Credit Jaysen Michael

Credit Joseph De Sciose

SIDEWALK FILM CENTER + CINEMA

WHAT: A nonprofit organization that promotes independent film and filmmaking

WHERE: 1821 Second Ave. N

COST: Prices vary

PRO TIP: Save time to grab a drink in the café while chatting with fellow film lovers.

The Sidewalk Film Center is all about building a community of filmmakers and film lovers. It offers monthly free events as well as educational programs that benefit everyone from film enthusiasts to professional filmmakers. It also offers filmmaker Q&A sessions and late-night indie movie screenings. There's always something going on to keep you engaged and inspired.

So, whether you're grabbing a drink, chatting with fellow moviegoers, or watching something you wouldn't find anywhere else, Sidewalk Film Center + Cinema is the place to be for anyone looking to experience the true creative pulse of Birmingham. It's the kind of spot you'll want to keep coming back to.

The Sidewalk Film Center in Birmingham is known for showcasing a diverse selection of films, from local and international features to documentaries and shorts.

A MUSICAL TRIBUTE TO CORNBREAD

Where can you find a tribute to an Alabama-born singer?

Cornbread isn't just a staple of Southern cuisine—it's also the nickname of an Alabama native and celebrated soul singer from the legendary group the Temptations. Born in 1937, Eddie Kendrick, famously known as Eddie Kendricks, rose to fame as a lead singer for the group, delivering timeless hits like "The Way You Do the Things You Do" and "My Girl."

Eddie Kendrick Memorial Park, dedicated on October 16, 1999, honors Kendricks's musical legacy and his enduring ties to his hometown. Located at the corner of Fourth Avenue North and 18th Street in Birmingham, the park features a striking bronze statue of Kendricks in mid-performance, crafted by local artist Ron McDowell. Surrounding the sculpture, granite panels are engraved with titles of the Temptations' greatest hits. Smaller sculptures represent the other members of the iconic group, and collectively, they create a heartfelt tribute to their impact on music history. Something you might not notice at first glance is that the singers' cuffs each have a letter inscribed on them, which, from left to right, spell out "BHAM," a subtle nod to Birmingham.

EDDIE KENDRICK MEMORIAL PARK

WHAT: Sculpture and garden paying tribute to a legendary singer

WHERE: Corner of Fourth Ave. N and 18th St.

COST: Free

PRO TIP: Parking is limited nearby, so consider pairing your visit with a walk through Birmingham's Civil Rights District.

Eddie Kendrick Memorial Park celebrates the voice that helped define an era. Courtesy of Mark Hilton

This small musical garden is located in Birmingham's Civil Rights District, making it a great starting or ending point for exploring the city's rich cultural and social history. Visitors can listen to recordings of Kendricks and the Temptations, learn about their impact on music, and reflect on the legacy of a hometown hero who continues to inspire.

Despite its small size, the Eddie Kendrick Memorial Park pays significant tribute to Kendricks and the Temptations.

STAINED GLASS SPLENDOR

Where can you experience some of the best acoustics in the city?

The Cathedral of Saint Paul, often referred to as St. Paul's Cathedral, is one of the many historic churches located downtown. Established in 1872, the parish's original church was located across from the current site on Third Avenue North. The present neo-Gothic structure, designed by Chicago architect Adolphus Druiding, was completed in 1893 and later elevated to cathedral status in 1969 with the creation of the Diocese of Birmingham.

THE CATHEDRAL OF SAINT PAUL

WHAT: A historic neo-Gothic cathedral

WHERE: 2120 Third Ave. N

COST: Free

PRO TIP: If you're visiting to experience the acoustics, try to catch one of the cathedral's musical performances.

One of the cathedral's most captivating features is its stunning stained glass windows. These windows not only enhance the interior's beauty but also narrate biblical stories and cast vibrant hues that shift with the changing daylight.

Beyond its visual splendor, the cathedral is known for its exceptional acoustics, which makes it a favored venue for musical performances, particularly choral and organ recitals. The recent installation of a new organ by the Noack Organ Company has further enriched its musical heritage. Many

---

The Cathedral of Saint Paul is a sought-after venue for musical performances due to its amazing acoustics.

Photo courtesy of Chris Pruitt

musical professionals agree the auditory experience inside the cathedral during services and concerts is unmatched.

An often overlooked aspect of the cathedral is its resilience and adaptability. Over the years, it has undergone several renovations, including the addition of air conditioning in 1955, structural repairs in 1972, and a comprehensive exterior restoration in 2015. With each change, parishioners work to preserve the cathedral's legacy for future generations.

The Cathedral of Saint Paul is a living chronicle of the city's cultural and spiritual evolution. Its blend of historical significance and artistic beauty makes it worth a visit.

A HERO WITHOUT A CAPE

Is it a bird? Is it a plane? Or could it be Batman?

Under the glow of Birmingham's streetlights, a sleek 1971 Ford Thunderbird prowled the avenues. Its owner wasn't just another motorist. To the people of Birmingham, he was Batman—a quiet, unassuming hero who never sought the limelight, but it somehow found him anyway.

For decades, Willie J. Perry, who became a local legend, dedicated his evenings to helping stranded drivers and passersby. Flat tires, dead batteries, empty gas tanks—it didn't matter. If you were in need, Batman was there, tools in hand and his Thunderbird ready to roll. His actions spoke louder than words, which earned him a place in the hearts of countless residents who encountered his kindness.

Perry's Thunderbird, known as the Batmobile Rescue Ship, became as iconic as the Batmobile itself. Unlike the fictional Batman of Gotham, Birmingham's version didn't wear a cape or hide behind a mask. Instead, he donned a gentle smile and a workman's determination. He embodied the spirit of selflessness that cities often need most.

Years after his passing in 1985, Perry's legacy lives on. In February 2024, he was immortalized in a mural that graces a wall in downtown Birmingham. The mural depicts him in his Thunderbird, a reminder of the impact one person can have

---

Birmingham's Batman, Willie J. Perry, dedicated his evenings to helping stranded drivers with a smile and his 1971 Ford Thunderbird. His actions earned him a place in the hearts of countless residents and a mural in downtown Birmingham.

Top: *A downtown mural celebrates Birmingham's own superhero. Courtesy of Pat Byington*

Bottom: *This is the actual car Willie J. Perry used to help stranded motorists. Courtesy of Jacob Blankenship/Bham Now*

BIRMINGHAM'S BATMAN

WHAT: Mural honoring the selfless acts of Willie J. Perry

WHERE: Magnolia Point building on the corner of Magnolia Ave. S and 23rd St. S

COST: Free

PRO TIP: Reflect on the legacy of Birmingham's Batman while you're there. It's not just a mural; it's a tribute to a man who made kindness his superpower.

when they dedicate their life to serving others. The mural is a testament to a man who made Birmingham better, one small act of kindness at a time.

The Thunderbird, as much a hero as its owner, carried its own remarkable legacy. After Birmingham's Batman passed, the car became a cherished relic of his life's work. It was displayed at the Southern Museum of Flight for many years. Later, it found temporary homes at the Alabama State Fairgrounds and a city garage near Birmingham-Shuttlesworth International Airport. In 2015, it moved to Old Car Heaven, a venue that celebrated classic automobiles, until the facility permanently closed in 2017.

Today, the car is kept safely in a family garage, a private tribute to a public hero. Though it no longer roams the streets of Birmingham, its story—and that of its owner—lives on.

The story of Birmingham's Batman inspires those who see the mural to lend a hand, pay it forward, and keep his legacy alive.

FLIPPERS, FLICKS, AND FUN

Where can you find Birmingham's best pinball players?

For more than 30 seasons, the Magic City Pinball League (MCPL) has been a fixture of Birmingham's gaming community. The league draws pinball enthusiasts from all over the area and currently has active participation from over 40 players. It has become a cornerstone of fun and competition for people of all ages and skill levels.

MAGIC CITY PINBALL LEAGUE

WHAT: A community of pinball enthusiasts

WHERE: Various locations

COST: Entry fee for the season

PRO TIP: Attend a few sessions as an observer to get a feel for the league's atmosphere, watch tournaments in action, and see the different skill levels.

Each Thursday night, pinball players gather at various homes in the Birmingham area, where they compete, learn, and bond over their shared love of pinball. The league runs in six-week seasons, and participants are split into two divisions to ensure that players of all skill levels have a fair and enjoyable experience. At MCPL, you'll find everything from seasoned pinball wizards to newcomers just discovering the thrill of the game. If you love pinball, there's a place for you in the league. MCPL also hosts tournaments once a month on a Saturday.

Interested in joining? It's easy! Simply attend one of the weekly meetings on Thursday nights to observe or participate. You can also join the league by signing up at the start of a new season. The league encourages people of all experience levels to get involved, and players can always reach out with questions through the league's social media page. Just search

The Magic City Pinball League hosts tournaments once a month. Courtesy of Alex Hoffman

for Magic City Pinball League on Facebook, where updates, event details, and registration information are regularly posted.

The Magic City Pinball League offers a unique opportunity to experience a quirky, vibrant part of Birmingham's story. It's the perfect way for pinball lovers to make their mark in the Magic City.

The Magic City Pinball League is a community of pinball enthusiasts that offers a fun and competitive environment for players of all skill levels.

SEEDS OF TRANSFORMATION

How is a farm transforming education and addressing food insecurity in Birmingham?

Jones Valley Teaching Farm (JVTF) began in 2007 with a bold idea: transform Birmingham's vacant lots into spaces of growth and learning. What started as a single urban farm has evolved into a citywide educational initiative, with seven Good School Food farms embedded in Birmingham City Schools. These farms act as outdoor classrooms where students engage in hands-on learning about agriculture, science, and healthy living.

One standout program is the Center for Food Education, where high school interns gain practical skills and career readiness in food systems. The center also hosts workshops, cooking classes, and community events. It's a valuable resource for residents and a launchpad for local food initiatives.

Beyond education, JVTF actively tackles food insecurity. Produce grown on the school farms is donated to local food banks or sold at student-run markets. This fosters entrepreneurship among students and brings fresh, affordable food to underserved communities.

Jones Valley Teaching Farm also helps teachers develop new and creative ways to engage their students. Many educators use the farms to create interdisciplinary lessons,

---

Jones Valley Teaching Farm is an example of how urban agriculture can transform communities. JVTF has not only created educational opportunities for students but also addressed food insecurity and fostered entrepreneurship.

Learning and nature grow together at Jones Valley Teaching Farm. Courtesy of T.K. Mc

blending STEM, arts, and humanities in creative ways. This approach not only enriches students' learning experiences but also demonstrates how urban agriculture can be a tool for systemic change.

Thanks to strong community support and partnerships, JVTF thrives, proving that urban farming is more than growing crops—it's about cultivating knowledge, sustainability, and hope for a healthier future. By equipping Birmingham's youth with these tools, Jones Valley Teaching Farm is sowing seeds of transformation that will yield benefits for generations.

JONES VALLEY TEACHING FARM

WHAT: A nonprofit organization in Birmingham focused on education, sustainability, and food access

WHERE: 701 25th St. N + seven teaching farms throughout the city

COST: Varies based on the season

PRO TIP: Schedule your visit ahead of time, especially if you're interested in one of the educational programs or workshops.

IT'S THE CLIMB

Where can you have the ultimate climbing experience in the Magic City?

Looking for an adrenaline-pumping adventure in Birmingham? Look no further than Birmingham Boulders, also known as B2. Birmingham Boulders is the ultimate playground for rock climbing enthusiasts. As the largest bouldering-specific facility in the area, it promises a unique and exhilarating experience for climbers of all skill levels.

Birmingham Boulders began downtown as First Avenue Rocks in 2009 and opened its current facility near Red Mountain Park in 2016. This new facility boasts state-of-the-art climbing walls and training equipment. The expansive training area is the largest of its kind in the country. It provides climbers with the resources they need to hone their skills and push their limits. In addition to bouldering, Birmingham Boulders offers yoga classes, youth teams, and climbing instruction courses. The facility even hosts private events, birthday parties, and summer camps.

Employees describe the atmosphere at Birmingham Boulders as welcoming and inclusive, which makes it easy for newcomers to feel at home and keeps experienced climbers coming back

BIRMINGHAM BOULDERS

WHAT: Indoor rock climbing gym

WHERE: 136 Industrial Dr.

COST: Check website for current prices.

PRO TIP: Visit on weekday afternoons for a more relaxed experience with fewer climbers.

Birmingham Boulders offers a unique and exhilarating experience for climbers of all skill levels.

Not only can you scale walls at Birmingham Boulders, but you can also take other classes and attend events here. Courtesy of Birmingham Boulders

for more. The community vibe is strong, with climbers of all ages and backgrounds coming together to share their passion for the sport.

So, if you're looking for a new adventure or a place to challenge yourself, head over to Birmingham Boulders. It's a place where the thrill of climbing meets the warmth of a supportive community. It is truly one of Birmingham's most unique attractions.

NOT YOUR AVERAGE BAR

THE HOUSE OF FOUND OBJECTS

WHAT: A distinctive cocktail bar featuring an eclectic blend of decor

WHERE: 2205 Second Ave. N

COST: Cover price varies depending on the time of arrival.

PRO TIP: At the House of Found Objects, you can get a custom cocktail by sharing your favorite flavors or personality traits with the bartender.

What hidden stories await at the House of Found Objects?

When you step into the House of Found Objects, you'll immediately notice that it's not your average bar—it's an immersive experience that blurs the line between art and nightlife. This one-of-a-kind establishment opened in 2022 and has quickly become a favorite destination for those seeking an unconventional night out.

The House of Found Objects lives up to its intriguing name, embracing a design ethos of whimsy and discovery. Here, you're immediately transported into an eclectic world filled with mismatched vintage furniture, vibrant murals, and an array of peculiar trinkets that seem plucked from a surreal treasure hunt. Owner Feizal Valli, a longtime Birmingham resident and art enthusiast, envisioned the space as a blend of a cozy speakeasy and an art gallery, and he succeeded brilliantly.

The cocktail menu is just as imaginative as the decor. The bartenders are known for crafting drinks that are as visually stunning

as they are delicious. Many of the signature drinks feature unexpected ingredients and theatrical presentations. The bar also offers an impressive selection of craft beers and wines that cater to every palate.

What makes the House of Found Objects unique is its commitment to storytelling. Many of the objects adorning the space are tied to local history, which makes it a scavenger hunt of sorts. Guests are encouraged to hunt for the hidden meaning of the objects. Look closely, and you might spot an old ticket stub from a bygone Birmingham theater or a piece of vintage railroad memorabilia nodding to the city's industrial roots.

If you're seeking an evening that's equal parts culture and fun, the House of Found Objects is a captivating adventure waiting to be discovered.

The House of Found Objects is where cocktails collide with curiosities. Here, you'll find unique, vintage, and eclectic pieces.

CAPTURE THE PAWN

Where can you play chess on an oversized chess board?

Close your eyes and imagine a chessboard. Now, think of the biggest one you've ever seen. I'd be willing to bet that what you're picturing isn't nearly as grand as the chessboard in Mountain Brook's Crestline Village. Here, the chess pieces are large and invite anyone passing by to make their move in this unique, interactive art display.

Located in front of City Hall, this oversized display features giant chess pieces and a massive board. Created by Villages Design Review Committee member and local artist Sally Legg over a decade ago, it has been a prominent part of the city's landscape. Originally placed at the old Mountain Brook City Hall, the chess set was so positively received by the community that it was installed as a permanent fixture at the new City Hall location. Although it was briefly removed during the COVID-19 pandemic, the chess set's return was met with enthusiasm from both city officials and residents. The community's fondness for the display is evident, with the area often bustling with children and adults of all ages engaging in friendly games.

Photos courtesy of the National Park Service

THE CHESS PIECES ART DISPLAY IN MOUNTAIN BROOK

WHAT: An interactive art display

WHERE: 55 Church St., Mountain Brook

COST: Free

PRO TIP: Pair your visit with a walk around the charming Mountain Brook Village nearby. Stop by Church Street Coffee & Books and try their signature cookie: the Breakup Cookie.

The chess pieces, some standing over 2 feet tall, are strategically arranged on a large black-and-white checkered board, inviting passersby to pause and play. The set is a fantastic mix of fun and creativity, offering a unique way for people of all skill levels to connect and enjoy a classic game.

What sets this chess set apart is its accessibility—free to play with and right in the center of a thriving village. It brings a sense of playfulness to the area while offering a chance for social interaction, making it a beloved feature of Mountain Brook. The installation was created as part of the city's ongoing commitment to public art and fostering a sense of community.

The chess pieces display invites the community to experience chess in a unique, hands-on way while also serving as a fantastic photo op.

A HEARTBREAKING LEDGE

Where can you have a picnic on a scenic escape?

Lover's Leap is a breathtaking historic overlook just minutes from Birmingham, located in the heart of Bluff Park. If you're not paying close attention, you might pass it by—but doing so would mean missing one of the most beautiful spots in the area. This iconic location offers more than just stunning views of the Cahaba Valley below; it's a place where natural beauty, history, and legend intertwine.

LOVER'S LEAP

WHAT: A historic and scenic overlook

WHERE: 586 Shades Crest Rd, Bluff Park, Hoover

COST: Free

PRO TIP: Early morning and sunset visits are especially captivating at Lover's Leap.

The overlook's rugged rocks are etched with inscriptions that date back over 150 years. These carvings—names, dates, and occasional short messages—are echoes of past visitors, each one adding a layer of human connection to the site. As you stand before these engravings, you can't help but imagine the stories of those who left their marks here.

Adding to Lover's Leap's mystique is the legend that gave the spot its name. As the story goes, a Native American maiden and her forbidden lover chose to leap from the cliff

---

According to legend, Lover's Leap got its name from a tragic love story involving a Native American maiden and her forbidden lover. A stone marker at the site commemorates their tale, giving this scenic overlook an air of romance.

Courtesy of Tim Carr

together rather than be faced with separation. A stone marker commemorates their tale, further deepening the site's sense of romance and history.

But the allure of Lover's Leap extends far beyond its legends. The panoramic views of the Cahaba Valley are unmatched. In fact, it's a popular location for photography, quiet picnics, or simply soaking in the beauty of Shades Mountain.

Lover's Leap is a timeless escape that invites visitors to reflect on its rich past and savor the serene present.

WALL OF DREAMS

What do you want to do before you die?

As you walk along the cobblestone streets of historic Morris Avenue in Birmingham, you might come across a colorful mural that stands out against the backdrop of old brick buildings. The Before I Die mural invites passersby to pause and reflect. Its bright chalkboard surface is filled with aspirations, dreams, and reflections from the community. This mural is part of a global art initiative designed to inspire individuals to think about the life they want to lead, what they wish to accomplish, and what they hope to leave behind.

The Before I Die project, created by artist Candy Chang, began as a single mural in New Orleans and has since blossomed into a worldwide phenomenon, with over 5,000 installations in more than 75 countries. Its purpose is simple: to engage people in meaningful conversations about life, purpose, and mortality. The mural features the prompt, "Before I die, I want to ______________," encouraging those walking by to grab a piece of chalk and fill in the blank. In Birmingham, the mural has become a canvas for the community, with people sharing their hopes, fears, and ambitions for the future.

This mural is so special because it fosters community connection. Local voices are woven into the fabric of the

BEFORE I DIE MURAL

WHAT: Interactive art installation

WHERE: 2070 Morris Ave.

COST: Free

PRO TIP: Bring a piece of chalk with you so you can contribute to the mural.

This interactive art installation fosters community connection as local voices contribute to the mural's evolving message.

Leave your mark on Birmingham at the Before I Die mural, a powerful public art installation inviting visitors to share their dreams, goals, and hopes.

piece, with people contributing to the mural's evolving message. The responses range from lighthearted wishes to deeply personal reflections, which is indicative of the human experience. When you encounter this art piece, you're witnessing a collective storytelling project that connects individuals through their shared hopes and dreams. The "Before I Die" mural is a profound and accessible experience for all who witness it.

CHASING WATERFALLS

Where can you chase waterfalls near the Magic City?

You might not think of waterfalls when you picture Birmingham, but just a short drive from the city center lies one of the area's hidden treasures: Turkey Creek Nature Preserve. This beautiful natural area is located in northeast Jefferson County and boasts some of the most varied ecology in central Alabama. It's a haven for nature lovers, adventure seekers, and those looking for a bit of respite from the bustle of the city.

The central attraction of the preserve is Turkey Creek Falls. The falls are easily accessible via a scenic trail that is suitable for hikers of all skill levels. The rushing waters tumble over smooth rocks into a crystal-clear pool below. It's a peaceful and serene spot to cool off on a warm day or simply bask in the natural beauty. The sound of the falls coupled with the lush green surroundings creates a tranquil escape from the noise of the nearby city.

Adding to Turkey Creek Nature Preserve's beauty and uniqueness is its role as a vital habitat for the vermilion darter, a vibrant, two-inch fish found nowhere else in the world. This rare species reinforces the ecological significance of the preserve and highlights the importance of its conservation efforts.

Beyond the falls, the preserve features a variety of trails. It's a perfect spot for hiking, picnicking, or simply relaxing and enjoying the beauty of Alabama's natural environment.

TURKEY CREEK NATURE PRESERVE & FALLS

WHAT: A 466-acre natural area diverse in ecology, scenic trails, and a waterfall

WHERE: Northeast Jefferson County

COST: Free, but donations are appreciated.

PRO TIP: Don't forget water shoes if you plan to explore the creek, as some of the best spots are just off the beaten path

Photos courtesy of Wally Argus

Turkey Creek Nature Preserve is a great spot for hiking, picnicking, or simply relaxing and enjoying the beauty of the natural environment.

IF THESE WALLS COULD TALK

Where can you explore a home that preserves Birmingham's black history?

History, resilience, and community empowerment—three things that summarize the Ballard House's purpose and mission. This stately two-story structure carries a rich legacy that stretches back over eight decades. Once the home of Dr. Edward H. Ballard and his family, the Ballard House has evolved into a living archive of Birmingham's African American heritage.

Built in 1940, the Ballard House originally served as a residence and a hub for African American professionals, activists, and educators during the height of segregation. Dr. Ballard, a respected physician and community leader, ensured the house was a safe space for discussions that shaped the fight for civil rights. The home's walls have witnessed countless conversations about justice, equity, and the future of Birmingham's African American community.

The Ballard House is a recognized symbol of the ongoing fight for civil rights. It is a proud member of the National Park Service African American Civil Rights Network and was named one of the "20 Alabama Civil Rights Sites to Watch" by the World Heritage Fund in 2018.

Courtesy of Wally Argus

Today, the Ballard House Project works to preserve this legacy by transforming the space into a community-centered venue that bridges the past and the present. It serves as a cultural museum and event space, hosting exhibits and programs that explore Birmingham's black history and culture. The project aims to educate and inspire, spotlighting stories often overlooked in mainstream narratives.

One of its unique features is its focus on oral history. By collecting and sharing personal stories, the Ballard House Project connects visitors with the voices of those who lived through pivotal moments in history, fostering a deeper understanding of the city's complex past.

Visiting the Ballard House is more than a historical tour; it's a journey into the heart of Birmingham's fight for justice and its enduring spirit of community. Whether exploring exhibits or attending events, guests leave with a profound sense of connection to this city's remarkable story of resilience.

THE BALLARD HOUSE PROJECT

WHAT: A cultural and historical preservation initiative

WHERE: 1420 Seventh Ave. N

COST: Free

PRO TIP: Check the Ballard House website or social media for upcoming events and exhibits.

MOBILE GREENERY SHOP

Where can you shop for lush greenery aboard a vintage bus?

You've heard of ice cream trucks and food trucks, but in Birmingham, there's a vehicle that caters to an entirely different craving—plants. Meet the plant bus, a mobile greenery shop brought to life by the House Plant Collective. What's a plant bus, you ask? Picture a vintage vehicle transformed into a lush, rolling oasis packed with a variety of houseplants, unique pots, and plant care essentials.

The House Plant Collective, founded in 2020, offers more than just a shopping experience; it delivers a green escape. What started as a plant bus has blossomed into a full-scale operation with a brick-and-mortar shop in the Avondale neighborhood. The shop specializes in curating plants that fit any space or aesthetic, from beginner-friendly succulents to striking, rare tropicals for seasoned plant parents.

The House Plant Collective's goal extends beyond selling plants—it's on a mission to make the joy of plants accessible

Photos courtesy of House Plant Collective

HOUSE PLANT COLLECTIVE

WHAT: A unique plant shop offering a mobile plant bus and a brick-and-mortar store

WHERE: 3621 Fifth Ave. S

COST: Prices vary depending on the plants and products.

PRO TIP: Follow the House Plant Collective on social media to track where the plant bus will pop up next.

to everyone in a fun and creative way. The plant bus travels to local events, farmers markets, and neighborhoods throughout Birmingham. Meanwhile, the brick-and-mortar location takes things to the next level with workshops, personalized plant consultations, and custom designs tailored for homes and offices.

HPC's commitment to sustainability and education is commendable. By prioritizing locally sourced and eco-friendly products, they promote environmentally conscious plant care. Both the shop and the plant bus serve as spaces to cultivate meaningful connections—linking people, plants, and the planet.

No matter whether you're looking to liven up your living room or start your first plant collection, the House Plant Collective delivers a unique experience that's as much about cultivating community as it is about growing greenery.

The House Plant Collective is a unique plant shop in that it offers a mobile plant bus and a brick-and-mortar store. The mission is to make the joy of plants accessible to everyone in a fun and creative way.

A LEGEND LIES HERE

Where can you pay tribute to one of the greatest football coaches in history?

It's pretty much a rule that if you live in Alabama, you have to pick a team—Alabama or Auburn. Whichever side you land on, you're likely familiar with the name Paul "Bear" Bryant. Known as one of the greatest football coaches in history, Bryant's legacy is cemented not only in sports but also in the culture of the state.

PAUL "BEAR" BRYANT'S BURIAL SITE

WHAT: Final resting place of Paul "Bear" Bryant

WHERE: Elmwood Cemetery

COST: Free

PRO TIP: Check the cemetery's map, as it's rather large.

In Birmingham's Elmwood Cemetery, beneath tall oaks and along quiet pathways, is Bryant's final resting place. His grave, marked by a simple plaque, is a humble tribute to a man whose impact was anything but small. Fans often visit to pay their respects, leaving behind mementos like hats, houndstooth-patterned items, and Alabama football memorabilia.

Bryant's story is one of grit and greatness. Born in rural Arkansas, he earned his nickname after wrestling a bear as a boy, a moment that foreshadowed his indomitable spirit. As head coach of the University of Alabama football team from 1958 to 1982, he led the program to six national championships

---

Despite his impressive accolades, Bryant's final resting place reflects his humility and connection to the community he loved.

Courtesy of Nathan Watson/Bham Now

and 13 SEC titles, earning 323 career wins—a record at the time of his retirement.

Yet, Bryant was more than his accolades. He was a symbol of resilience, discipline, and leadership, values that resonated with Alabamians and secured his place as an icon. His grave, understated yet meaningful, reflects his humility and enduring connection to the community he loved.

WHISPERS OF THE PAST BEHIND VELVET CURTAINS

What hidden tales lie behind Birmingham's most iconic marquee?

Many who pass by the historic Alabama Theatre see its dazzling marquee, but few realize the whispers of history that linger within its walls. Behind the velvet curtains and beneath the flickering lights, secrets of a bygone era wait to be uncovered. The grandiose architecture of the building holds stories as interesting as its charm.

Built in 1927 by Paramount Studios, the Alabama Theatre was designed to showcase the studio's latest films. But its role quickly expanded beyond the world of cinema. It became a stage for dreams, hosting the annual Miss Alabama pageant and echoing with the laughter of children at the weekly Mickey Mouse Club. It evolved into a cultural heartbeat of Birmingham, where stories—both on and off the screen—came to life.

One of the theater's most captivating features is its "Mighty Wurlitzer" organ, affectionately dubbed "Big Bertha." This magnificent instrument, with its pipes cleverly concealed in

---

The Alabama Theatre was once called the "Showplace of the South" and can seat over 2,500 guests.

Left: *Photo courtesy of Jack Boucher via Wikimedia Commons*

Opposite: *Photo courtesy of Carol Highsmith via Wikimedia Commons*

ALABAMA THEATRE

WHAT: A historic theater built in 1927

WHERE: 1817 Third Ave. N

COST: Ticket prices vary by event.

PRO TIP: Arrive early to take in the theater's stunning architecture.

ornate box seats, was integral to the theater's ambiance during the silent film era. Remarkably, the organ remains operational today and offers audiences a nostalgic auditory experience that hearkens back to the golden age of cinema.

Architecturally, the Alabama Theatre is a melting pot of styles. Its interior boasts a blend of Mission and Spanish Revival motifs, interspersed with Egyptian and Moorish designs. When patrons enter, they are greeted by a two-story anteroom adorned with mirrored walls and a star-shaped chandelier embellished with over 8,000 crystals. Adjacent lounges further showcase the theater's eclectic design, featuring Middle Eastern and Italian influences.

In 1993, the Alabama Theatre was designated as the official state historic theater of Alabama, underscoring its significance in the state's cultural and architectural history.

Today, the Alabama Theatre hosts everything from classic films to live performances, yet many people overlook its fascinating details and rich history. To preserve its cultural importance, officials added the theater to the National Register of Historic Places in 1979, ensuring future generations can experience its charm and grandeur.

REV UP YOUR ENGINES

Where can you watch fast cars charge toward the finish line?

Just an hour east of Birmingham, right next to the Talladega Superspeedway, is a collection of racing history housed in the International Motorsports Hall of Fame. While the speedway often takes center stage, many overlook the rich legacy housed in this museum, just a few steps away.

Since 1983, this museum has preserved some of the most significant artifacts in motorsports. Beginning in 1990, the Hall of Fame began inducting the pioneers and innovators who pushed racing to new heights. The first ceremony, held on July 25 of that year, celebrated 20 of motorsports' greatest figures, and set the stage for the museum's continued growth. On the following day, a ribbon-cutting ceremony unveiled a new 15,000-square-foot building, cementing the Hall's status as a premier destination for motorsports fans.

INTERNATIONAL MOTORSPORTS HALL OF FAME

WHAT: Largest and fastest NASCAR track in the United States

WHERE: 3198 Speedway Blvd., Lincoln

COST: Ticket prices vary.

PRO TIP: Ask a staff member for insider stories about the legends behind the cars for an even deeper appreciation of the motorsports history.

The museum is filled with legendary cars, memorabilia, and exhibits honoring groundbreaking drivers and the unforgettable moments that have defined racing. Historic cars sit alongside modern machines, illustrating the sport's evolution. Visitors can explore interactive displays that offer a taste of racing simulations, making it an interactive experience.

Courtesy of Tennessee Wanderer

A visit to the International Motorsports Hall of Fame is a journey through the evolution of motorsports and its impact on the world. It brings the high-speed, high-stakes world of racing to life in a way that will leave you with a new appreciation for the sport.

The International Motorsports Hall of Fame is right next to the Talladega Superspeedway. This awesome museum is packed with legendary cars, famous drivers, and memorabilia that have made motorsports what it is today.

REACH FOR THE STARS

Where can you deepen your understanding and appreciation for astronomy without going to outer space?

Why settle for the moon when you can reach the stars and beyond? In the Birmingham area, the moon and the stars might feel a little closer than you think at the Christenberry Planetarium. Located at Samford University, this unique place provides an immersive experience for space enthusiasts and curious minds alike. Opened in 2001 as part of the university's Sciencenter (Center for Science and Religion), the Christenberry Planetarium is the largest planetarium at a teaching institution in Alabama. It boasts a 40-foot domed ceiling, which enhances its realistic and awe-inspiring presentations of the night sky. The planetarium's state-of-the-art projection system includes an optomechanical star projector, re-creating the cosmos with remarkable detail.

Named after the Christenberry family, whose generous contributions made the planetarium possible, the facility serves as a testament to the family's dedication to promoting science and education. One of the planetarium's many highlights is its wide range of educational programs. These programs are designed for both students and the general public. The venue offers interactive shows that explore astronomy, stars, planets, and other celestial phenomena. Visitors can enjoy educational

---

Be sure to visit the Leslie S. Wright Fine Arts Center while on Samford's campus, where you can explore its impressive collection of art, often overlooked by many despite the center's reputation for hosting concerts and performances.

CHRISTENBERRY PLANETARIUM

WHAT: Largest planetarium at an Alabama teaching institution

WHERE: 800 Lakeshore Dr., Homewood

COST: Admission is free, but certain special events may have a fee.

PRO TIP: Check the special events calendar ahead of time to plan your visit.

Photo courtesy of Christenberry Planetarium

experiences such as "Star of Bethlehem" during the holiday season or concerts that use the planetarium's technology to create stunning visuals set to music. The venue is used not only by Samford students but also by local schools and community groups for field trips and special events. It makes science accessible and fun for people of all ages.

The Christenberry Planetarium is also a key component of Samford's commitment to integrating the sciences with other fields of study, particularly in encouraging young people to pursue careers in STEM (science, technology, engineering, and mathematics). Its cutting-edge technology brings the universe to life and invites visitors to explore the mysteries of space in an interactive and educational way.

PROVISIONS & PANINIS

Where can you grab a sandwich and shop for cute kitchen decor in the same place?

Part quirky café, part general store, General in Forest Park is a unique blend of local charm and inviting warmth that captures the spirit of Birmingham. This spot is a cozy gathering place, where the line between a café and a general store blurs. You can enjoy a cup of locally roasted coffee while browsing an eclectic collection of items ranging from vintage books and handmade gifts to carefully curated pantry staples.

The menu at General is an array of delicious bites that are great for breakfast or lunch. Whether you're in the mood for a warm bowl of oatmeal, fresh avocado toast, or a hearty sandwich, there's something for everyone. The seasonal offerings often highlight local produce and ingredients in an effort to curate fresh and flavorful options. Paired with the artisan coffee, it's the perfect place for a casual meal or a light snack.

The atmosphere at General is relaxed. With both indoor and outdoor seating options, visitors can enjoy the fresh air on the charming patio, especially on sunny days. The outdoor space is a favorite for those looking to study, meet friends, or catch up on work while sipping a latte. Inside, the inviting decor creates a space ideal for reading, small meetups, or leisurely conversations.

Stop in and grab a cup of coffee and a treat while browsing for unique items at General.

GENERAL

WHAT: Café and general store

WHERE: 3813 Clairmont Ave. S.

COST: Varies

PRO TIP: Take advantage of the outside seating on a sunny day.

General's prime location, right in the heart of Forest Park, makes it a convenient and welcoming spot for locals and visitors. Whether you're stopping in for a quick coffee or spending a few hours relaxing with friends, General provides the ideal backdrop for both work and play.

General Birmingham in Forest Park is a quirky spot where history and charm collide. It's as full of personality as the neighborhood itself.

A GIFT THAT ENDURES BEYOND LIFE

How can you keep giving long after you're gone?

Some people give it their all—literally. The Donor Memorial at the University of Alabama at Birmingham (UAB) is a tribute to those who did just that, donating their bodies to medical science for research and education. Located on UAB's campus, this intriguing memorial combines creativity with profound meaning.

DONOR MEMORIAL

WHAT: A memorial honoring those who have donated their bodies to medical science

WHERE: Volker Hall, 1670 University Blvd.

COST: Free

PRO TIP: Just a short walk from the Donor Memorial is the UAB Sculpture Garden. Stop by to see the unique outdoor art installations.

You have to be intentional to find this striking metallic sculpture. It stands in a concrete space that might otherwise go unnoticed. Positioned between the UAB School of Medicine and the Lister Hill Library of the Health Sciences, this memorial serves as a tribute to some generous individuals. These people, even in death, have offered the ultimate gift—continuing to serve a vital purpose in advancing medical education. Through their selflessness, they have made a lasting impact on the training of future healthcare professionals, quite literally giving of themselves to ensure that others can learn and grow.

The Donor Memorial doesn't just celebrate the generosity of those who contributed to medical research; it also serves as a reminder of the impact these donations have had. UAB students and faculty have used these gifts to push the boundaries of science and education. The memorial's aesthetic

Donor Memorial pays tribute to those who have donated their bodies to medical science.

contrasts invite people to pause, reflect, and appreciate the lasting influence of those who made such compassionate choices.

In the anatomy lab, the donors' identity is protected, but at the memorial, their names are proudly etched for families and visitors to appreciate. Donor Memorial is worth the trek. Take a moment to stop by, reflect on the legacy of giving, and perhaps even snap a photo of this striking and moving tribute.

This memorial is a striking metallic sculpture that stands between the UAB School of Medicine and the Lister Hill Library. It serves as a tribute to generous individuals who have made a lasting impact on medical education.

COOLEST PLACE IN TOWN

Did you know you can go ice skating just outside Birmingham?

If you want to build a snowman, Birmingham probably isn't the place to go. But, if you want to go ice-skating, you can slide over to the Pelham Civic Complex and Ice Arena. It's just a quick 20-minute drive from downtown, and it's the perfect spot to glide across the ice and skate to your heart's content. This unexpected year-round winter wonderland boasts not one, but two National Hockey League-sized ice rinks.

The complex caters to all skill levels. It offers public skating sessions where families can bond over laps around the rink or giggle through a few wobbly falls. First-timers can take lessons from skilled instructors who are experts in transforming nervous shuffles into confident glides. For those

PELHAM CIVIC COMPLEX & ICE ARENA

WHAT: Ice-skating arena and event venue

WHERE: 500 Amphitheater Rd., Pelham

COST: Public skating admission fee

PRO TIP: Check the online schedule before visiting to confirm public skating hours.

Pelham Civic Complex & Ice Arena is home to the Birmingham Bulls—the city's Professional Hockey League team.

with competitive ambitions, the arena also offers hockey leagues and figure-skating programs. You might even catch a synchronized skating team rehearsing routines that look like something straight out of a winter fairy tale.

The complex is also home to the Birmingham Bulls, the city's professional hockey team. The Bulls bring high-energy games and an electric atmosphere to the arena. Whether you're a die-hard fan or a first-time attendee, catching a Bulls game is a must for sports lovers.

But ice sports aren't the only draw. The Pelham Civic Complex doubles as a vibrant event space. It hosts everything from expos and weddings to corporate gatherings. Its expansive banquet facilities and dedicated event staff make it a popular choice for large and small celebrations.

So, while Birmingham might not see much snow, Pelham ensures that the joy of a wintery escape is always within reach—no snow boots required.

In addition to ice sports, the Pelham Civic and Ice Complex has welcomed the Harlem Globetrotters and showcased several theatrical ice performances.

THE MILL THAT NEVER MILLED

Where in the city has time stood still?

In the quiet confines of Jemison Park in Mountain Brook, you can catch a glimpse of a landmark that looks like it's straight out of a story book. That site is the Old Mill. The Old Mill has charmed visitors for decades and remains one of the most photographed sites in the area. With its rustic stone facade, ivy-draped walls, and wooden waterwheel, the Old Mill is hidden in plain sight. In fact, if you're not from the area, it's likely that you'll pass right by it and not even know it's there.

The mill was constructed in the 1920s, and a surprising fact is that it was never a working gristmill. Instead, it served as an architectural centerpiece for Mountain Brook's early

THE OLD MILL

WHAT: A charming, historic structure

WHERE: Mountain Brook's Jemison Park, 2615 Mountain Brook Pkwy.

COST: No public access

PRO TIP: You can see the mill from the public walking trails.

Though the Old Mill is now a private residence, it continues to be a cherished local landmark. Courtesy of Wally Argus

development, embodying the English countryside aesthetic that defines much of the community's charm. Though the mill has undergone restoration efforts over the years, it's historic allure is still very present.

Not only is the Old Mill a visual delight—it's also steeped in nostalgia. For many Mountain Brook residents, it's the backdrop of childhood memories: lazy afternoons spent wandering the nearby trails, family picnics along Shades Creek, and seasonal photo shoots to commemorate milestones. The lush greenery and serene creek-side setting make it a favorite spot of respite for those seeking a pause from the bustle of the nearby city.

The Old Mill is a private residence, so there's no public exploring allowed. However, you can stroll along the shaded pathways, listen to the gentle sound of the creek, and take in the timeless beauty of a site that has stood as a symbol of Mountain Brook for nearly a century.

The Old Mill's iconic image was cherished so deeply that it once adorned the badges and cruisers of the Mountain Brook Police Department.

BIRMINGHAM'S GILDED GUARDIAN

Where can you find a golden statue in Birmingham?

High above Birmingham's skyline, a golden figure has symbolized progress and innovation for nearly a century. Standing 23 feet tall, *Electra*, a gilded bronze statue, has crowned the Alabama Power Company's original office building since 1926. Initially named *The Divinity of Light*, the statue, created by New York sculptor Edward Field Sanford Jr., was soon affectionately nicknamed *Electra*, reflecting her electrifying presence.

ELECTRA STATUE

WHAT: Gilded bronze statue

WHERE: 600 18th St. N

COST: Free

PRO TIP: Bring a camera with a zoom lens for detailed shots of this iconic figure.

Architect William T. Warren convinced Alabama Power's directors to install *Electra* rather than a large electric sign. While some questioned placing a nude figure on the roof, Warren assured them the statue would become a timeless emblem. The board agreed, and *Electra* has since embodied Alabama Power's progressive vision.

Her popularity extends beyond admiration—she inspired the whimsical cartoon series *The Love Story of Vulcan and Electra*, imagining romantic escapades between Birmingham's two iconic statues.

Vulcan isn't the only iconic statue in Birmingham. *Electra* has been a beloved and talked-about landmark for nearly a century.

Electra *shines as a symbol of energy, strength, and Birmingham's industrial legacy. Courtesy of David Brossard*

In 1988, a replica of *Electra*, crafted from Italian *statuario* marble, was unveiled in the atrium of Alabama Power's new corporate tower. The two statues now bridge the company's legacy, linking its art deco roots with its modern identity.

Electra continues to shine as a true "Divinity of Light" watching over the Magic City.

A HIDDEN NATURAL ESCAPE

Did you know you can scale boulders near Birmingham?

Several nooks and crannies scattered around the city offer a bit of calm, and some are more hidden than others. Moss Rock Preserve in Hoover is one such place. This 349-acre sanctuary of unspoiled nature and outdoor adventure provides the perfect escape to relax and reconnect with the outdoors. Best of all, it's just a few minutes from downtown Birmingham.

Known for its rugged boulder fields, cascading waterfalls, and diverse ecosystems, Moss Rock Preserve offers a peaceful retreat for hikers, climbers, and nature enthusiasts. One of the preserve's most remarkable features is its sandstone boulder formations, which attract rock climbers from across the Southeast. These massive stones, shaped and smoothed over hundreds of years, create a natural playground for both beginner and experienced climbers.

The preserve also boasts numerous trails that offer a mix of leisurely strolls and more challenging hikes. Many pathways lead to tranquil creeks, shaded woodlands, and open meadows, which come to life during wildflower season.

If scaling rocks isn't your thing, Moss Rock Preserve is still well worth a visit. The soothing sound of its waterfalls

---

This 349-acre sanctuary of unspoiled nature and outdoor adventure is known for its rugged boulder fields, cascading waterfalls, and diverse ecosystems. Hikers, climbers, and nature enthusiasts love this peaceful retreat just minutes from downtown Birmingham.

Photos courtesy of Wally Argus

MOSS ROCK PRESERVE

WHAT: Nature preserve

WHERE: 617 Preserve Way, Hoover

COST: Free

PRO TIP: Visit in the fall for cooler weather and breathtaking views of autumn foliage.

creates the perfect soundtrack for a day spent outdoors. The preserve is also home to an incredible array of diverse ecosystems, including rare plant species like the Alabama croton, which thrives here due to the unique geology and ongoing conservation efforts.

Beyond its natural beauty, Moss Rock Preserve serves as an educational space. Interpretive signs along the trails highlight the significance of the area's flora, fauna, and geological formations. It's a learning experience for visitors of all ages.

Accessible yet beautifully secluded, Moss Rock Preserve feels like a world away from the city; yet, it's just a stone's throw from downtown Birmingham. It's an inviting place to reconnect with nature and discover one of Birmingham's most beautiful landscapes.

THE GOLDEN DOME

What is the gold onion dome you see when merging onto I-459 from I-20?

If you've ever merged onto I-459 from I-20/59, you've probably noticed the gold onion dome peeking above the trees. That lustrous dome belongs to the building once known as the Zamora Shrine Center, an iconic structure that has stood in Irondale for decades.

FORMER ZAMORA SHRINE CENTER

WHAT: Former meeting space for the Zamora Shriners

WHERE: 3521 Ratliff Rd., Irondale

COST: Not open to the public

PRO TIP: This building was recently purchased by the City of Irondale. Since the former Zamora Shrine Center isn't open for exploration, take a scenic drive by it and the nearby Statue of Liberty replica for a quick and unique sightseeing combo.

For many years, the Zamora Shrine Center was the heart of the local Shriners community. It served as the meeting place for the Zamora Shriners, a Masonic fraternity. It became a symbol of fellowship and charity for all who knew it. Outside of being a gathering space for Shriners, the building was also a beloved venue for community events. Dozens of high school proms, weddings, and banquets were held at the center. The distinctive architecture made it a memorable backdrop for many celebrations.

However, as the years passed, the building's use began to dwindle, and the Shriners made the decision to sell it. In 2022, the City of Irondale took a significant step toward preserving the building's legacy when it announced plans to purchase the former Zamora Shrine Center. The city aims to revitalize the space, bringing new life to the historic structure while preserving its architectural charm. Irondale officials have

Courtesy of Pat Byington

hinted at transforming the building into a community center, with potential uses ranging from civic events to cultural activities.

The purchase of the Zamora Shrine Center marks a new chapter in the building's history. As Irondale moves forward with its plans, the iconic onion dome will continue to stand as a symbol of both the city's rich past and its promising future.

This iconic building is now owned by the City of Irondale and is set to be revitalized into a community center.

HOME OF ALABAMA'S GREATEST ATHLETES

Where can you find Alabama's top athletes in one place?

Though many Birminghamians know about the Alabama Sports Hall of Fame (ASHOF), many are unaware of its true significance. Many pass by the striking building without realizing that it houses one of the most respected sports institutions in the country. Widely regarded as a model of excellence, the ASHOF honors the incredible athletic talent and achievements of Alabama's finest, both past and present.

Founded in 1967, the Hall of Fame's mission is to preserve the legacy of Alabama athletes while inspiring future generations. It has more than 400 inductees and spans every sport imaginable—from football and baseball to tennis and auto racing. The exhibit showcases the achievements of legendary figures like Bo Jackson, Hank Aaron, and Willie Mays, alongside lesser-known but equally important figures in Alabama sports history.

Visitors to the ASHOF are greeted by memorabilia, including trophies and jerseys, and interactive displays that highlight the accomplishments of inductees. The hall is a testament to Alabama's rich sports history and the talented athletes who helped shape it.

The ASHOF has earned national recognition and is often called the "model of excellence." It is widely respected for preserving Alabama's athletic legacy. As Birmingham grows,

---

Celebrate Alabama's sports legends at this downtown museum honoring the state's greatest athletes.

ALABAMA SPORTS HALL OF FAME

WHAT: Museum that celebrates the state's athletic achievements

WHERE: 2150 Richard Arrington Jr. Blvd. N

COST: Prices vary.

PRO TIP: When you visit the Alabama Sports Hall of Fame, make sure to check out the statues of legendary coaches Bear Bryant and Shug Jordan right outside the museum. These statues honor two of the most iconic figures in Alabama's rich sports history and are a great spot for photos.

Top: *The Alabama Sports Hall of fame houses photos and other memorabilia celebrating the state's athletic history. Courtesy of Chris Pruitt*

Bottom: *Seal outside Alabama Sports Hall of Fame. Courtesy of Sterling Graham*

the hall continues to be an important part of the city's identity. Sports fans and history lovers alike will enjoy this unique look at the state's athletic achievements.

EAGLE FLIGHT IN THE CITY

How is Auburn University demonstrating innovation through its expansion into Birmingham?

Your eyes were not deceiving you if you thought you saw an Auburn University sign in downtown Birmingham. Many people have wondered why Auburn University has seemingly popped up in downtown Birmingham. This isn't a building specifically for classes, but rather an extension office of sorts where Auburn can provide innovative opportunities for students, professors, and business leaders. The building opened in the downtown innovation district and has seamlessly integrated Auburn's legacy of academic excellence with Birmingham's growing business and technology communities.

AUBURN IN BIRMINGHAM

WHAT: Auburn University's new facility in downtown Birmingham

WHERE: 2013–15 Fourth Ave. N

COST: Free to visit, but reservations are required for tours or room bookings.

PRO TIP: Book a tour by appointment for an in-depth visit.

One fascinating aspect of this building is its history. It's housed in the former Hood-McPherson Building, an iconic fixture in downtown Birmingham where furniture was once assembled and sold. After a six-year renovation, the 44,000 square foot, six-story building now provides instructional, collaborative, and administrative space for various Auburn programs.

This expansion is a representation of Auburn's commitment to workforce development, regional growth, and educational excellence. By fostering direct collaboration with local businesses and industries, Auburn is helping to address workforce needs in fields like technology, engineering, and

Auburn University may be two hours away from Birmingham, but it now has a presence in the city.

business. The new building also creates additional opportunities for Auburn students to engage with professionals and innovators.

Interestingly, the building also includes Auburn's Urban Studio, a teaching and outreach program that gives students hands-on experience in the environment of downtown Birmingham. This program has contributed to some of Birmingham's most popular redevelopment projects, such as the Pepper Place farmer's market and Railroad Park green space.

Ultimately, the Auburn in Birmingham building marks a new chapter for the university. It merges its proud academic history with the dynamic future of Birmingham. This expansion is an essential part of Auburn's strategy to make a meaningful impact in Alabama while shaping the next generation of leaders and thinkers.

The six-story Auburn in Birmingham facility features adaptive classrooms, collaborative meeting spaces, and innovative areas designed to foster interdisciplinary connections among faculty, students, and researchers.

WINGS OVER BIRMINGHAM

Where can you learn about Alabama's aviation history?

On the east side of Birmingham, on the grounds of the Birmingham-Shuttlesworth International Airport, there lies a place where aviation and history collide: the Southern Museum of Flight. This aviation hub showcases more than 100 aircraft, making it one of the largest aviation museums in the Southeast. There, you'll find everything from warplanes to modern marvels. Every display invites you to explore humanity's endless quest to conquer the skies.

SOUTHERN MUSEUM OF FLIGHT

WHAT: Aviation museum

WHERE: 4343 73rd St. N

COST: Prices vary.

PRO TIP: Guided tours are available at an additional cost.

The museum, founded in 1966, goes beyond showcasing planes. It weaves together tales of courage, ingenuity, and

Discover aviation's rich legacy at the Southern Museum of Flight, where iconic planes greet visitors with stories of the skies. Courtesy of Wally Argus

local pride. You'll see exhibits honoring the Tuskegee Airmen, Alabama's own aviation heroes, and even the quirky story of the "Huff-Daland Duster," the world's first crop-dusting plane. On the outside of the museum, massive military jets and helicopters are on display, giving a tactile glimpse of aviation history.

Interactive simulators take the museum experience to new heights. No pun intended. Ever dreamed of being a fighter pilot? These stations let you soar through the skies or try your skills at landing a plane.

One of the Southern Museum of Flight's standout exhibits tells the story of a B-25 bomber famously displayed in Birmingham's Fountain Heights neighborhood. This captivating piece of local history reflects the museum's unique appeal. It blends significant historical moments with relatable, community-centered storytelling.

The Southern Museum of Flight houses an impressive collection of over 100 aircraft, including rare and historic planes like a full-size replica of a Wright Flyer.

FIGHTING FOR A FAIRER TOMORROW

How did Bethel Baptist Church shape the Civil Rights Movement?

Resilience, courage, and faith—these are words often used to describe the historic Bethel Baptist Church in Collegeville. Established in 1904, Bethel is more than a place of worship; it's a living beacon of the Civil Rights Movement and remains an active church today, with a dedicated congregation of approximately 400 members.

Under the leadership of Rev. Fred Shuttlesworth, who became pastor in 1953, Bethel Baptist gained national recognition as a focal point for racial justice. Shuttlesworth, a fearless advocate for equality, co-founded the Alabama Christian Movement for Human Rights after the NAACP was outlawed in Alabama. Bethel became a headquarters for mass meetings, strategy sessions, and activism, earning its place as a cornerstone in the fight against segregation.

The church's legacy was established in the face of grave danger. Bethel endured multiple bombings in the late 1950s and early 1960s, including a Christmas Day bombing in 1956. These attacks, meant to instill fear, only solidified Shuttlesworth's resolve and galvanized the community's commitment to justice. Despite the repeated acts of violence,

BETHEL BAPTIST CHURCH

WHAT: Former headquarters for Rev. Fred Shuttlesworth and the Alabama Christian Movement for Human Rights

WHERE: 3233 29th Ave. N

COST: Admission varies for tours.

PRO TIP: Schedule ahead to ensure access. Stop by the Fred Shuttlesworth mural at the Birmingham-Shuttlesworth International Airport and read the plaques to learn more about his fearless leadership.

Bethel Baptist Church is listed as a National Historic Landmark. Visit the church's website to schedule a tour. Courtesy of Jet Lowe

the church's mission endured. Shuttlesworth became a national figure of resilience.

Today, Bethel Baptist Church is a National Historic Landmark and part of the Birmingham Civil Rights National Monument. It has been the subject of numerous interviews and documentaries, drawing attention to its pivotal role in the civil rights movement. Educational tours of the church are offered, allowing visitors to walk through the sanctuary and parsonage, see where meetings took place, and see where artifacts are preserved as powerful symbols of faith and activism.

Walking the grounds of Bethel, one can almost feel the indomitable spirit of its past.

Bethel Baptist Church is a National Historic Landmark that played a pivotal role in the Civil Rights Movement under the leadership of Rev. Fred Shuttlesworth.

THE 4,700

Is it true that bodies are buried on the grounds of the Birmingham Zoo?

There is way more at the Birmingham Zoo and Botanical Gardens than what meets the eye. On these 200 acres lies a history that many visitors may not realize. The land was once home to Red Mountain Cemetery, a burial ground established in 1888 as Birmingham's first public cemetery. Over 4,700 individuals were laid to rest here, including some of the city's poorest residents, as the cemetery primarily served those unable to afford private burial plots.

In the mid-20th century, the city began repurposing the land, transforming it into what we now know as the Birmingham Zoo and Botanical Gardens. However, records of Red Mountain Cemetery were poorly kept, and efforts to relocate the graves were far from thorough. Today, archaeologists estimate that hundreds, possibly thousands, of bodies remain beneath the zoo and surrounding areas.

In 2023, the zoo acknowledged this history when plans to expand its exhibits brought archaeologists to the site to recover and relocate human remains. The effort shed light on the forgotten lives buried there, including victims of the Spanish flu pandemic and other late 19th- and early 20th-century tragedies. This somber task also served as a reminder of the city's often-overlooked history of neglecting its most vulnerable communities.

Walking through the zoo today, it's humbling to imagine the layers of history beneath your feet. What was once a

---

Before becoming home to the Birmingham Zoo and Botanical Gardens, this land was the site of the former Red Mountain Cemetery.

This marker stands at the spot of the former Red Mountain Cemetery, which is now the home of the Birmingham Zoo and the Birmingham Botanical Gardens.

place of quiet rest has become an attraction, filled with families, school groups, and conservation efforts. It's a reminder that Birmingham's past is always present, even in the most unexpected places.

FORMER RED MOUNTAIN CEMETERY

WHAT: A former public cemetery

WHERE: On the grounds of the Birmingham Zoo and Birmingham Botanical Gardens

COST: Free to explore the public areas of the Botanical Gardens; entry fees apply to the Birmingham Zoo.

PRO TIP: A few old markers from Red Mountain Cemetery remain scattered throughout the zoo and botanical garden.

HOME IN THE HEART OF THE CITY

Why is First Presbyterian Church known as the heartbeat of downtown Birmingham?

Downtown Birmingham is not short on beautiful churches rich in history. First Presbyterian Church is one of those churches. Sitting at the corner of 21st Street and Fourth Avenue North, FPC has been a steadfast presence in the city since 1872. From its early beginnings as the Old School Presbyterian Church in Elyton, the congregation moved to the bustling new city of Birmingham, building the first church in the downtown area.

First Presbyterian Church's sanctuary was built in 1888 and reflects the congregation's enduring faith and evolving needs. Over the years, it has been enhanced with intricate stained glass windows and updates to accommodate its growing membership. Adding to its historical significance, the Rushton Memorial Carillon—a historic set of 37 bells—was installed in 1924. This was the first carillon in Birmingham and only the third in the United States, making it a remarkable piece of the church's legacy.

FIRST PRESBYTERIAN CHURCH

WHAT: Historic church

WHERE: 2100 Fourth Ave. N

COST: Free; donations are encouraged to support ministries.

PRO TIP: Visit a Sunday service at 11 a.m. and enjoy the timeless sound of the Rushton Memorial Carillon, which continues to ring every Sunday at noon.

The Rushton Memorial Carillon at First Presbyterian Church is a piece of Birmingham's cultural and spiritual story. It was gifted in 1924 by James Franklin Rushton, a well-known local businessman, in memory of his father, William J. Rushton. Back then, it wasn't uncommon for prominent

Courtesy of Wally Argus

families to leave their mark by supporting churches and the arts, and this gift was a perfect example. The 37 bells were cast by the renowned John Taylor & Co. in England. For decades, the sound of the carillon rang out through the city, turning the church into a landmark of music and memory.

But this church is more than its architecture. First Presbyterian played a critical role during pivotal moments in Birmingham's history, particularly the Civil Rights Movement. Under the leadership of Dr. Edward V. Ramage, the church became a symbol of courage and conviction.

Throughout its history, First Presbyterian has been dedicated to service, addressing social challenges from homelessness to payday lending. Even as downtown Birmingham experienced decline, the church never wavered in its mission, remaining a "Home in the Heart of the City."

First Presbyterian Church is a stunning historic landmark known for its beauty and rich history. Don't miss the sound of its bells, which still ring out, adding a nostalgic touch to the city's atmosphere.

WALKING THROUGH HISTORY

Where can you walk a trail that tells a story?

Birmingham's story is incomplete without acknowledging its pivotal role in the Civil Rights Movement. While many visitors are familiar with the Birmingham Civil Rights Institute, the Civil Rights Heritage Trail offers a broader, deeper narrative. This self-guided tour connects over 100 stops. It blends iconic landmarks with lesser-known sites to paint a picture of resistance, resilience, and change.

The trail isn't just a series of historical markers—it's a walk through time. It winds through Birmingham's streets, uncovering the people and places that shaped a movement. One of the most notable stops is Kelly Ingram Park, where courageous demonstrators faced police dogs and fire hoses during protests. Today, the park serves as a living monument that features powerful sculptures capturing the raw emotion of the fight for equality.

Nearby, you'll find the 16th Street Baptist Church, a somber reminder of the 1963 bombing that claimed the lives of four young girls. Across the street, the historic A. G. Gaston Motel once served as a meeting ground for civil rights leaders like Dr. Martin Luther King Jr. and Rev. Fred Shuttlesworth as they strategized for change.

There are many other less mentioned yet equally important

With over 100 stops on this educational trail, you'll want to take time to plan your route before setting out on your journey.

Each stop on the Birmingham Civil Rights Heritage Trail offers a deeper understanding of the struggles and triumphs of the Civil Rights Movement in Birmingham. Courtesy of Andre Natta

BIRMINGHAM CIVIL RIGHTS HERITAGE TRAIL

WHAT: A self-guided tour that takes you through over 100 significant sites in Birmingham

WHERE: Downtown Birmingham

COST: Free

PRO TIP: Download the trail map and app, which provide additional context and details about the sites.

stops along the trail. The Loveman's Department Store marker tells the story of lunch counter sit-ins that quietly but powerfully challenged segregation. Then there's the Birmingham Jail, where Dr. King wrote his famous letter that still resonates today.

Walking the Birmingham Civil Rights Heritage Trail is a history lesson. But it is also a profound act of remembrance and reflection. The trail celebrates the bravery of ordinary people who brought extraordinary change, reminding us all that the fight for justice continues.

Some powerful, yet often overlooked stops on the Birmingham Civil Rights Heritage Trail include the Lynching Memorial, Dynamite Hill, and the Birmingham Pledge Monument.

Photo courtesy of Wally Argus

SOURCES

Welcome to the Magic City
Site visit, April 27, 2024

al.com/bhammag/2018/11/then-now-magic-city-rotary-trail-sign.html

Where Veterans Day Was Born
Site visit, November 8, 2024

nationalveteransday.org/history

World's Largest Cast Iron Statue
Site visit, October 4, 2024

visitvulcan.com

encyclopediaofalabama.org/article/vulcan-statue-and-vulcan-park

Lady Liberty Overlooking Liberty Park
bhamwiki.com/w/Liberty_National_statue

atlasobscura.com/places/statue-of-liberty-replica-alabama

A Symbol of Industrial Growth
Site visit, June 13, 2024

Interview with Tyler Malugani, Education Coordinator, June 13, 2024

World's Largest Motorcycle Museum
Site visit, February 20, 2025

barbermuseum.org/the-barber-story

The Heaviest Corner on Earth
Site visit, October 8, 2024

atlasobscura.com/places/heaviest-corner-on-earth-birmingham

Urban Nature Preserve
encyclopediaofalabama.org/article/ruffner-mountain

Symbol of the Civil Rights Movement
Site visit, June 16, 2024

nps.gov/places/sixteenth-street-baptist-church.htm

Oldest Baseball Park in America
Site visit, November 8, 2024

Weeks, J. D. (2007). *Birmingham.* Arcadia Publishing, 2007.

rickwood.com

Birmingham's Oldest Hotel
historic-hotels-lodges.com/2018/05/the-redmont-hotel.htm

al.com/living/2016/01/history_of_the_1925_redmont_ho.html

From Railroad Depot to Historical Hub
Site visit, October 26, 2024

Brown, Alan. *Haunted Birmingham.* The History Press, 2009.

Italian Temple in Birmingham
Site visit, January 4, 2025

vhal.org/sibyl-temple

Birmingham's Oldest Rescue Mission
Site visit, June 13, 2024

bbmission.com/history

Japanese Garden in Birmingham
Site visit, October 26, 2024

japanese-city.com/calendar/events/index.php?com=location&lID=1879

Historic Masonic Temple Building
nps.gov/places/masonic-temple-building.htm

Romanesque Playhouse at Caldwell Park
Bennett, J. R. *Historic Birmingham & Jefferson County.* Birmingham-Jefferson Historical Society, 2008.

bhamnow.com/2018/04/03/208286

Century-Old Legacy Car Dealership
Site visit, December 3, 2024

280.chevyman.com/about-us/our-100-year-history

Bennett, J. R. *Historic Birmingham & Jefferson County.* Birmingham-Jefferson Historical Society.

History on a Cobblestone Road
Site visit, October 6, 2024

bhamwiki.com/w/Morris_Avenue

First Public Library in the City
Site visit, September 7, 2024

bhamwiki.com/w/Linn-Henley_Research_Library

Jazz in the Magic City
jazzhall.com/our-mission

Alabama's Oldest Restaurant
Site visit, October 26, 2024

birminghamoriginals.org/thebrightstar

First School in the City
Crider, Beverly. "Birmingham's First School" in *Lost Birmingham.* The History Press, 2013.

Finest Art Collection in the Southeast
Site visit, October 4, 2024

birmingham365.org/organization/birmingham-museum-of-art

1840s Greek Revival Mansion
Site visit, October 4, 2024

Lewis, J. M. "Museum Review of the Arlington Historical House and Gardens, Birmingham, Alabama." *The Saber and Scroll Journal* 11, no. 4 (2023).

Resting Place for Birmingham's Pioneers
Site visit, November 8, 2024

encyclopediaofalabama.org/article/oak-hill-cemetery

Legendary Cafeteria Line
Site visit, October 30, 2024

nikiswest.com/about-us.php

Hey, Batter Batter
Site visit, June 6, 2024

birminghamnslm.org

State-of-the-Art Auto and Engine Manufacturer
Site visit, April 10, 2024

John Long, email message to author, October 24, 2024

hondanews.com/en-US/honda-corporate/channels/company-facts

Follow the Green Trail
Site visit, September 28, 2024

Cuhaj, J. *Hiking Alabama: A Guide to Alabama's Greatest Hiking Adventures* 3rd ed. Morris Book Publishing, LLC, 2007.

A Whisper Beneath the Whiskey
al.com/life/2019/07/with-its-bar-and-tasting-room-complete-dread-river-distilling-co-is-finally-ready-for-the-public.html

dreadriver.com/about-us

bhamwiki.com/w/Underground_river

Sustenance in the City
Site visit, August 24, 2024

pepperplacemarket.com/about

The Mining Years
exploringalabama.org/trails/crusher-trail

alabamarecreationtrails.org/trail/crusher-trail

Haven for Injured and Orphaned Animals
Site visit, November 8, 2024

alabamawildlifecenter.org

Center for Iron and Steel Production
encyclopediaofalabama.org/article/iron-and-steel-production-in-birmingham

Thanks for the Memories
Site visit, October 26, 2024

atlasobscura.com/places/museum-of-found-memories-at-reed-books

Boutique Bed & Breakfast
Email conversation with Miranda Callatrello, October 29, 2024

buckcreekbnb.com

Once-Tallest Skyscraper in the City
abandonedsoutheast.com/2017/05/27/city-federal

Fast Lane Fantasy
Site visit, February 20, 2025

Interview with Michael Gary, Porsche Sport Driving School, January 21, 2025

porschedriving.com/birmingham/faq

Tell Me a Story
Site visit, August 17, 2024

atlasobscura.com/places/the-storyteller-fountain

alstate.guide/metropolitan/jefferson/birmingham/storyteller

Treehouse Full of Books
Site visit, October 15, 2024

vestavialibrary.org/faqs

Where Water Meets History
bwwb.org/business/CahabaMuseum

bhamwiki.com/w/Cahaba_Pump_Station

Spirits in the Magic City
Site visit, January 25, 2025

bhamwiki.com/w/Redmont_Distilling_Company

redmontvodka.com/about

Longest-Surviving Greek-Owned Hot Dog Stand
gusshotdogs.com/history

A Tribute to Birmingham's Culinary Icon
Site visit, August 3, 2024

al.com/life/2019/11/new-sculpture-honors-alabama-chef-frank-stitt.html

A Stroll Through Artistic Masterpieces
uab.edu/aeiva/about

Scrap-Iron Story of Culture and Heritage
birminghamtimes.com/2021/10/inside-joe-minters-renowned-african-village-in-america

Bistro in Birmingham
alabama.travel/places-to-go/chez-fonfon

fonfonbham.com/about

Blooming Books and Blossoms
Site visit, August 3, 2024

jclc.org

Dirigible Landing Post
Site visit, December 26, 2024

atlasobscura.com/places/thomas-jefferson-zeppelin-mooring-mast airships.net/blog/alabama-pretends-dirigible-tower-hotel-didnt

abandonedalabama.com/thomas-jefferson-hotel

Rainy Day Revolution
encyclopediaofalabama.org/article/mary-anderson

Café with a Side of Quirk
Site visit, November 7, 2024

al.com/entertainment/2017/05/15_things_you_might_not_know_a_3.html

Lights, Camera, Birmingham!
Site visit, January 24, 2025

sidewalkfest.com/about

A Musical Tribute to Cornbread
Site visit, April 3, 2024

rockandrollroadmap.com/places/miscellaneous/other-u-s-locations-miscellaneous/eddie-kendrick-memorial-park/#google_vignette

Stained Glass Splendor
magiccityreligion.org/2021/11/29/the-cathedral-of-saint-paul

stpaulsbhm.org

A Hero Without a Cape
al.com/news/2024/02/birmingham-batman-who-helped-motorists-with-his-1971-ford-thunderbird-honored-in-mural.html

Flippers, Flicks, and Fun
Email conversation with Frank Williamson and Alex Huffman, December 4, 2024

Seeds of Transformation
jvtf.org/our-sites

It's the Climb
bhamboulders.com/history

Email conversation with Melysa Zippel, January 2, 2025

Not Your Average Bar
Site visit, December 17, 2024

bhamnow.com/2022/11/09/an-inside-look-at-the-house-of-found-objects-a-new-bar-opening-nov-16

Capture the Pawn
Site visit, December 13, 2024

Telephone interview with Sam Gaston, city manager of Mountain Brook, December 11, 2024

A Heartbreaking Ledge
hooverhistoricalsociety.org/history-of-bluff-park

bluffparkal.org/heathers_corner_lovers_leap.htm

Wall of Dreams
Site visit, November 8, 2024

beforeidieproject.com

bhamnow.com/2019/04/05/before-i-die-i-want-to-______-here-are-your-responses-to-the-new-birmingham-mural-on-morris-ave-plus-how-you-can-help-paint-the-next-one

Chasing Waterfalls
Spencer, Thomas. *Five-Star Trails: Birmingham: 35 Beautiful Hikes in and Around Central Alabama*. 2nd ed. Menasha Ridge Press, 2021.

If These Walls Could Talk
Voice of Alabama. "The Ballard House." World Moments Fund, March 2020.

youtube.com/watch?v=Lghj1XmYfSQ

ballardhouseproject.org/about

Mobile Greenery Shop
houseplantcollective.com/about-us

Watts, Jessica, email to author, January 2, 2025

A Legend Lies Here
findagrave.com/memorial/1739/paul-bryant

encyclopediaofalabama.org/article/paul-bear-bryant

Whispers of the Past Behind Velvet Curtains
Site visit, January 29, 2025

gardenandgun.com/articles/the-souths-surprising-saturday-night-fever-connection

al.com/entertainment/2013/06/movie_director_john_badham_who.html

Rev Up Your Engines
birminghamal.org/listings/talladega-superspeedway

encyclopediaofalabama.org/article/talladega-superspeedway

Reach for the Stars
Site visit, January 25, 2025

samford.edu/news/2005/Samford-to-Dedicate-Christenberry-Planetarium

thesamfordcrimson.com/2023/10/31/christenberry-planetarium

Provisions & Paninis
Site visit, May 6, 2024

facebook.com/generalbham?mibextid=ZbWKwL

A Gift That Endures Beyond Life
Site visit, January 10, 2025

atlasobscura.com/places/donor-memorial

Coolest Place in Town
pelhamalabama.gov/1023/Ice-Arenas

The Mill That Never Milled
gardenandgun.com/feature/the-home-tucked-inside-a-historic-mill-house

hmdb.org/m.asp?m=83922

Birmingham's Gilded Guardian
alabamanewscenter.com/2016/05/17/electra-statue-turns-90-years-old-remains-birmingham-beacon

A Hidden Natural Escape
hooveral.org/214/Moss-Rock-Preserve

alabama.travel/places-to-go/moss-rock-preserve

exploresouthernhistory.com/mossrock.html

The Golden Dome
Site visit, July 12, 2024

bhamnow.com/2022/06/08/irondale-to-purchase-former-zamora-shrine-center

gadsdenshrineclub.org/zamora-shrine-center.html

bhamwiki.com/w/Zamora_Shrine_Center

Home of Alabama's Greatest Athletes
encyclopediaofalabama.org/article/alabama-sports-hall-of-fame-ashof

ashof.org/about/mission-statement-and-history

birminghamal.org/listings/alabama-sports-hall-of-fame

Eagle Flight in the City
Site visit, and tour September 10, 2024

theplainsman.com/article/2024/06/in-the-heart-of-birmingham-auburns-new-building-enhances-opportunities

aubham.auburn.edu

Wings over Birmingham
Site visit, January 11, 2025

Sirois, K. *Insider's Guide to Birmingham.* Morris Book Publishing, LLC, 2011.

encyclopediaofalabama.org/article/southern-museum-of-flight

Fighting for a Fairer Tomorrow
thehistoricbethel.org/history

nps.gov/places/thehistoric-bethel-baptist-church.htm

The 4,700
Site visit October 26, 2024

al.com/news/2023/12/archaeologists-begin-moving-graves-to-make-way-for-new-birmingham-zoo-exhibit.html

cbs42.com/news/cbs-42-investigates/more-than-4000-people-buried-under-birmingham-zoo-and-botanical-gardens

al.com/news/birmingham/2023/08/who-are-the-people-buried-on-the-birmingham-zoo-grounds.html

Home in the Heart of the City
Site visit, September 6, 2024

fpcbham.org/partners

Walking through History
alabama.travel/places-to-go/birmingham-civil-rights-heritage-trail

hmdb.org/results.asp?Search=Series&SeriesID=689

birminghamcivilrights.com/civil-rights-trail-markers

INDEX

Photo courtesy of Wally Argus

Dread River Distilling Co.